"Sarah has provided just the right amount of depth and a plethora of practical strategies which won't cost the earth and feel realistic in the primary classroom. Easily navigable, the book can be dipped into as needed by busy staff looking for rapid responses."

Pooky Knightsmith, Child and Adolescent Mental Health Expert

"Sarah is a passionate practitioner who puts the child at the heart of everything she does. She is well researched and has shared her practical knowledge and skills in this book so that more children can benefit. A book that is easy to dip into when necessary, I have no doubt that this will be an extremely useful reference for primary teaching staff to support and include children with social, emotional and mental health challenges and enable them to be successful in the school environment."

Cath Kitchen, OBE, Chair of the National Association for Hospital Education

"This practical and user-friendly resource is a must have for every primary school practitioner who is seeking to support the well-being of our most vulnerable children and specifically those with social, emotional and mental health needs. It has been written by a practitioner who really knows what works and what ensures that everyone can flourish in the learning context. The use of case studies, reflection points and specific evidence-based strategies makes this a very accessible resource and one which will generate confidence for anyone new to the profession who is seeking to gain a deeper understanding of mental health needs and develop their practice in this area."

Tina Rae, Child Psychologist and Author

"Teachers and support staff working with children with social, emotional and mental health needs will find this book invaluable. It provides practical strategies and insights for supporting children's development and creating a safe and inclusive classroom. The book is divided by diagnosis, profile, or need, making it easy for teachers to find relevant information. Sarah uses her 20 years of education experience to offer practical solutions for those without comprehensive SEMH training. This book will help reduce exclusions and support SEMH children's transition to adulthood."

Abigail Hawkins, FCCT, SENsible SENCO

"This book is invaluable for anyone involved in supporting children with SEMH (social, emotional and mental health) needs. It covers the SEMH relevant to primary school pupils, recognising that behaviour is a way of communicating difficulties with emotional regulation. The book is laid out in a clear and logical way, with information about each condition, and practical tools and strategies which Sarah has drawn together from her 20 years in education. She also includes a list of story books which are aimed at pupils experiencing trauma, bereavement etc, and those around them."

Fiona Johnson, SENCO and SEN Consultant

ALL ABOUT SEMH

All About SEMH is an accessible and informative guide for primary school teachers, designed to increase their understanding of social, emotional and mental health needs, and to enhance their toolkit with practical, evidence-informed strategies to support children in their care.

The book unpicks key terminology and debunks myths and misconceptions, enabling teachers to more easily understand some of the challenges for learners with SEMH needs. It then explores a range of key areas, including anxiety, attachment, bullying and self-harm, and focuses on practical strategies and adaptations that can be made in every classroom. *All About SEMH* includes:

- A comprehensive introduction to social, emotional and mental health needs, and the surrounding terms and policies.
- Practical strategies tailored to different conditions to help provide targeted support to primary school learners.
- Case studies and worked examples to illustrate points in the book, supporting behaviour recognition and developing reader understanding.
- Discussion on different behaviour patterns in school and at home, with the voices of parents of children with SEMH woven throughout.
- Easy to dip in and out of chapters with signposting to further research, resources and support.

This accessible guide is a valuable resource to empower primary educators, increasing their knowledge and understanding of SEMH, and providing a range of practical strategies to support every learner in their class. It will be essential reading for all primary school educators, SENCOs and parents who are supporting children with SEMH needs.

Sarah Johnson is the founder of Phoenix Education Consultancy, which helps educational establishments to understand what they are doing well and looks at addressing gaps to improve their service. She previously worked in both primary and secondary mainstream education, including as director of inclusion for a large primary school, and as head of a Secondary Pupil Referral Unit.

ALL ABOUT SEND
Series Advisor: Natalie Packer

All About SEND provides busy teachers and SENCOs with essential guidance and practical strategies to effectively support learner with special educational needs and disabilities. Each accessible and informative book focuses on a common area of need and explores key traits and terminology, debunks myths and misconceptions, and introduces readers to a range of easy-to-implement ideas for practice and concrete solutions to everyday challenges.

ALL ABOUT AUTISM
A Practical Guide for Primary Teachers
Lynn McCann

ALL ABOUT AUTISM
A Practical Guide for Secondary Teachers
Lynn McCann

ALL ABOUT DYSCALCULIA
A Practical Guide for Primary Teachers
Judy Hornigold

ALL ABOUT SEMH
A Practical Guide for Primary Teachers
Sarah Johnson

ALL ABOUT SEMH
A Practical Guide for Secondary Teachers
Sarah Johnson

ALL ABOUT SEMH

A PRACTICAL GUIDE FOR PRIMARY TEACHERS

Sarah Johnson

Routledge
Taylor & Francis Group

LONDON AND NEW YORK

Designed cover image: © Getty Images

First published 2024
by Routledge
4 Park Square, Milton Park, Abingdon, Oxon OX14 4RN

and by Routledge
605 Third Avenue, New York, NY 10158

Routledge is an imprint of the Taylor & Francis Group, an informa business

© 2024 Sarah Johnson

British Library Cataloguing-in-Publication Data
A catalogue record for this book is available from the British Library

ISBN: 978-1-032-22566-1 (hbk)
ISBN: 978-1-032-22565-4 (pbk)
ISBN: 978-1-003-27309-7 (ebk)

DOI: 10.4324/9781003273097

Typeset in Interstate
by Deanta Global Publishing Services, Chennai, India

CONTENTS

FOREWORD

All teachers are teachers of learners with special educational needs and disabilities (SEND). Those professionals who work in truly inclusive schools will understand that SEND is everyone's responsibility. However, the situation has not always been like this. When I started my teaching career 30 years ago, learners who had additional needs were more likely to be seen as the responsibility of the special educational needs coordinator (SENCO). As the person in the school who 'held' the SEND knowledge and expertise, the SENCO would often be a lone force in championing, and meeting, the needs of this particular group of learners.

The picture in education is somewhat different today. The profile of the children and young people we teach continues to change. The impact of the COVID pandemic, for example, has led to an increase in those identified with gaps in their learning or with mental health concerns. The number of learners with complex needs being educated within mainstream schools also continues to rise. As professionals, we now have a greater awareness and understanding of some of the challenges our learners face and, as a result, are more determined to do our best to support them to achieve. We understand that this cannot be the role of one person – the SENCO – alone. Every teacher needs to be a teacher of SEND.

Teaching learners with SEND may be one of the most rewarding things you ever do in your classroom. When you observe a learner who has really struggled to grasp a new idea or concept finally achieve their lightbulb moment, it's all the more sweeter knowing the amount of effort they have put in to get there. However, teaching learners with SEND can also be one of the most challenging aspects of your career. In a 2019 survey[1] carried out by the Department for Education (DfE) in England, the level of confidence amongst teachers in supporting learners with SEND was reported as very low. Relevant professional development in this area is, at best, patchy; only 41% of the teachers surveyed by the DfE felt there was sufficient SEND training in place for all teachers.

So how do we overcome this challenge? Evidence suggests that the best place to start is through the delivery of inclusive, high quality teaching (HQT). As the Education Endowment Foundation (EEF) report[2] tells us, there is no magic bullet for teaching learners with SEND, and to a great extent, good teaching for those with SEND is good teaching for all. This means we need to develop a repertoire of effective teaching strategies such as scaffolding, explicit instruction and use of technology, then use these strategies flexibly to meet the needs of individuals or groups of learners.

Although a focus on effective HQT in the classroom is the starting point, some learners will require more specific teaching methods to meet their individual needs. There is no substitute for really getting to know a child or young person so you can fully understand their personal strengths, potential barriers to learning and what works for them in the classroom. However, it can still be helpful for us as professionals to develop a more general understanding of some of the common areas of need we are likely to come across and to have a range of strategies we can try implementing within our practice. This is where All About SEND can help.

The All About SEND series of books aims to support every teacher to be a teacher of SEND. Each book has been designed to enable teachers and other professionals, such as support staff, to develop their knowledge and understanding of how to effectively promote teaching and learning for those with identified areas of need. The books provide essential information and a range of practical strategies for supporting learners in the classroom. Written by expert practitioners, the guidance has been informed by a wealth of firsthand experience, with the views of children and young people with SEND and their parents taking centre stage.

In this book, *All About SEMH*, author Sarah Johnson provides a fascinating insight into the complexities of some of the social, emotional and mental health (SEMH) needs that an increasing number of our children are facing today. Having worked across a wide range of educational, youth and health settings, Sarah has vast experience in supporting children by reducing and removing social and emotional barriers to help them access education. As Director of Phoenix Education, she supports practitioners, school leaders, multi-academy trusts and local authorities to ensure every child can participate in, and enjoy, their education. In *All About SEMH*, Sarah encourages the reader to reflect on their own practice and consider how they may support children with SEMH needs to be included in the classroom and beyond.

Thank you for choosing to read this book and for embracing the challenge of responsibility: every teacher is a teacher of SEND.

Natalie Packer
SEND Consultant, Director of NPEC Ltd.
@NataliePacker

NOTES

1 https://assets.publishing.service.gov.uk/government/
  uploads/system/uploads/attachment_data/file/1063620
  /SEND_review_right_support_right_place_right_time_
  accessible.pdf, p. 42.
2 https://educationendowmentfoundation.org.uk/education
  -evidence/guidance-reports/send.

ACKNOWLEDGEMENTS

Thank you to my daughters: Octavia, Astrid and Iris. My oldest daughter was instrumental in looking through sections of the book and letting me know about her own experiences and strategies that have supported her, whilst Astrid and Iris, as babies, helped me reflect and consider development from the practical experiences of being a new mother.

Thank you to my mum, Janette, who has supported me unreservedly and made sure that I valued education.

To my brother, Warren, who continually demonstrates to me the power of resilience but also the ability to change his life around and support others. He is a testament to how finding a love of education at any age can shape your future for the better.

To my husband, Daniel, who put up with late nights and early mornings as I typed away writing this whilst also acting as a sounding board to explore ideas and approaches.

To those whom I work with and who have guided me with ideas, thoughts and sense checking. Liz Hunt has been a great 'sense checker' from her psychological perspectives as well as her strategic understanding of special educational needs and disabilities.

To those who are already respected in their fields and continue to share their experiences, their values and moral purpose that I hope to emulate in my own work and approach: Cath Kitchen, Dr Pooky Knightsmith and Dr Dan Owen. You have been and will continue to be incredible in helping me see the bigger picture and to look beyond schools and think about the role of schools within the wider community.

Finally, but certainly importantly, to those parents/carers and their children in sharing their experiences and providing their feedback to each section. Throughout the book I wanted to make sure that a parent would be happy for their child to be spoken about in the way that I had. Thank you for looking over what I wrote and helping me to talk about children in a nuanced and kind way.

ACRONYMS

ADD	attention deficit disorder
ADHD	attention deficit hyperactivity disorder
APA	American Psychiatric Association
ASC	autistic spectrum condition
ASD	autistic spectrum disorder
DfE	Department for Education
DSED	disinhibited Social Engagement Disorder
DSH	deliberate self-harm
DSM	*Diagnostic and Statistical Manual of Mental Disorders*
EBD	emotional behavioural difficulties
EBSA	emotionally based school avoidance
EDA	extreme demand avoidance
FASD	foetal alcohol spectrum disorder
NHS	National Health Service
OCD	obsessive-compulsive disorder
PANDAS	paediatric autoimmune neuropsychiatric disorders associated with streptococcal infections
PANS	paediatric acute-onset neuropsychiatric syndrome
PDA	pathological demand avoidance
SEMH	social, emotional and mental health
SEND	special educational needs and disabilities
RAD	reactive attachment disorder
UK	United Kingdom
UNICEF	United Nations International Children's Emergency Fund
UNCRC	United Nations Convention on the Rights of the Child

Part 1

INTRODUCTION

INTRODUCTION

THE PURPOSE OF THIS BOOK AND HOW YOU MIGHT USE IT

The purpose of this book is to provide an introductory guide for teachers and support staff to develop strategies to help children that have been identified as having social, emotional and mental health (SEMH) difficulties. This book is specifically aimed at those supporting children who are between the ages of 4 and 11 years.

To help you be able to find information when you need it, the chapters of the book are divided into different diagnoses, profiles or needs. The idea is that you can choose to either read the book from cover to cover or focus on a specific area that you would like extra support with.

Whilst special educational needs and disabilities (SEND) has many overlaps and children are complex, this book is about SEMH. For the ease of teachers and interested parties, this book serves those who would like to pick up a book, and think about their practice and how it may support children in being included in classroom activities and broader school life. The other books in this series and the knowledge contained therein will likely have significant overlaps and helpful information that may influence and inform the reader.

I have worked in education for 20 years in both primary and secondary school environments. This has included being a class teacher in a range of settings. I know only too well the challenge of balancing the needs of over 30 children whilst planning and teaching Citizenship and Personal, Health and Social Education. Or the different and sometimes competing needs of teaching children in the primary school curriculum. I have had the joy of

DOI: 10.4324/9781003273097-2

being the director of inclusion for a large primary school and provided strategic guidance in supporting children who found being in school and the class difficult. I have also been a form tutor for a large secondary school in London, with the associated challenges of teaching and pastoral care in a multicultural inner-city area.

I will start with the premise that teaching children can be incredibly hard. This is in terms of planning, consideration of the different requirements and pressures from the children themselves. Coupled with considering the demands and needs of key stakeholders such as parents/carers, senior leadership teams, the wider community and the range of accountability measures that might be in place, teaching is beyond that which happens in the classroom environment but extends into a range of other facets that require consideration. Some shorthand phrases that you may be aware of and underpin your work include *safeguarding*, *child protection*, *accessibility*, and *relationships*. These all underpin and provide structure to not just our subject knowledge but also to how children can flourish and feel safe in the classroom environment.

As a teacher or someone who regularly supports children, you may be acutely aware of these pressures, some of which are competing in nature. Depending on your geographical location and where you have trained, you may espouse infrequent and unstructured training on how to support the children who need your expertise the most.

Whilst training to be a teacher, and this experience is likely to be echoed by others, I felt ill-prepared for the diversity of needs within the classroom environment. Instead, the training offered to me was an afternoon training on SEND (dyslexia in this instance), and it had little or no practical suggestions on how to support children that did not fit within the narrow scope of the university's definition of SEND.

I was poorly equipped for the classroom environment despite having had a year in the classroom directly working with children during my training. The focus of my training was on subject content, producing lesson plans and curriculum sequencing for most children that I may see in my teaching career; in other words, those children that we may define as 'mainstream' or 'typical' of a class. This meant that I struggled with how to plan effectively for the range of children's needs. Whilst those children with behavioural, learning or attention needs may be seen as 'outliers', as with any career where you meet hundreds and thousands of children, those 'outliers' mount up to a significant number. You are likely to want to ensure that you support all children to learn and flourish in your classroom, not just those that meet a narrow definition of being a 'typical pupil'. I suspect as you read this you are similar to me in that you want to make your lessons impart key knowledge, build understanding and captivate children's interests.

My training happened nearly two decades ago. I am hopeful that if you have recently undertaken training in education that your experiences do not echo mine, and, instead, reading through this book forms a companion to your growing professional body of knowledge. It may even be that this book is on the reading list of your university or another professional body where you are undertaking training. If this is the case, then you are already in a position where you have had more guidance than my own training. I hope this book saves you some time and many mistakes, as well as igniting your curiosity to support all children's needs in the classroom.

Depending on where you are teaching or supporting children, there will be a range of terms that may describe children with difficulties that make it hard to access education due to the way they behave. You may have heard the following phrases in discussions and policy documents:

- social, emotional and mental health needs
- challenging behaviour
- behavioural difficulties
- at risk of exclusion
- emotional behavioural difficulties

You may have heard other terms such as:

- naughty
- poorly behaved

- inattentive
- inappropriate
- violent
- aggressive

In this book, the term 'social, emotional and mental health' is used, as it encapsulates both externalised behaviour (what you might be able to see in the classroom environment and what might be seen as disruptive) and internalised behaviour (how a child feels about being within the classroom and wider school environment).

Within the United Kingdom, SEMH needs are understood to be a specific SEND that is characterised by difficulty making and maintaining friendships, attending to and listening to the teacher, and expressing emotions in a way that is manageable in the classroom environment.

Some of these behaviours and challenges may permeate within other parts of the child's life such as at home, and relationships outside of school and within their local community. However, it is important to recognise this is not always the case, and the differing demands and structures of these environments may mean that some things that we see in school are not reported within other environments and vice versa. Indeed, the case may also be the opposite and you may hear reports from parents/carers about difficult situations that you do not recognise within the school environment. There is much criticism from parents and organisations around the disbelief in their experiences in the home environment when a teacher utters the phrase "they are fine at school".

As a teacher or other educational professional, you might hear about or see for yourself a range of behaviours such as:

- not listening to a teacher's instructions
- not speaking out loud to an adult or other children and young people
- being distracted and finding it hard to attend to the lesson content

- what appears to be an extreme emotional response to situations (tearfulness, aggression)
- refusal to attend school
- destroying school property
- destruction of own work
- shouting at others
- seeming sad or withdrawn

Meeting the needs of children with SEMH is important; it is important because all children and staff should feel safe and content at school. It is not just about the children who may demonstrate concerning behaviour and what we may define as SEMH needs, but it is also about those children within the school community who may find that their own learning is disrupted by others. The feelings of adults who teach and support those children are also a central concern of this book, as being knowledgeable and feeling empowered with strategies will also support teachers.

Further to this is the idea of the rights of the child. The United Nations Convention on the Rights of the Child enshrines the rights of the child to access education, and there are no caveats or conditions applied to that. Supporting children by reducing and removing any barriers to education is a way of ensuring children can access education.

Supporting children with SEMH needs is vital in helping them have their needs met within the school environment, reducing exclusions (both suspensions and permanent exclusions) and supporting them in becoming citizens who are economically active and belong to their communities. In addition, meeting children's needs and having a work environment for staff where they feel valued and supported in decision-making is important for staff retention.

Ultimately, the purpose of this book is about supporting those who work with children who may demonstrate some of the aforementioned behaviours. It can be used to 'dip in': you can turn to a specific chapter to find out more about specific SEMH needs, in order to consider and utilise practical strategies to implement within the class and within a school (for example, moving from one classroom space to another, during playtime or other unstructured times).

This book is not meant to dictate how things must be done, but one that kindles an interest, enthusiasm and creative exploration on helping children learn, whatever the barriers are to that learning.

THE EVOLUTION OF THE TERM 'SEMH'

As suggested earlier there is a range of ways in which SEMH needs have been referred to in education discourse, not just globally but historically within the UK. A factor with the use and interpretation of the SEMH need is complicated depending on where you have trained or are reading this from. You might be used to other catchall terms that try to group, understand and explain types of behaviour that may be externalised in behaviour that isn't better explained by neurodiversity (such as autistic spectrum conditions, specific speech and language disorders or learning difficulties). It is also important to recognise how neurodiversity, or a child's understanding of the world around them, may also significantly influence how they engage with others, how they feel emotionally and how they express these things. SEMH as an encompassing term attempts to simplify behaviours we might see but does little to really help us understand and provide support for children with diverse needs who might all sit within this umbrella term.

Focusing on the UK policy landscape, SEMH is a relatively new term having been used within the SEND Code of Practice (Special educational needs and disability code of practice 0–25 years, 2015). This indicated a shift from the previous term 'behavioural emotional and social difficulties (BESD)' and prior to this 'emotional behavioural difficulties (EBD)'.

This shift in terminology marked growing concerns that BESD focussed unduly on the externalised behaviour rather than underlying difficulties, with EBD being used instead to describe some of the presenting behaviours of children. In the move towards a change in the categorisation of special educational needs under the new SEND Code of Practice (Department for Education, Department for Health, 2022, p. 85), the term SEMH joined the descriptors of needs:

- communication and interaction
- cognition and learning
- sensory and/or physical needs

In recent statistics relating to how many children have special educational needs in England, the data suggests that 208,916 pupils are identified as having SEMH needs with 49,525 of those pupils having been issued an Educational Health Care Plan that recognises this (Office for National Statistics, 2022).

The SEND Code of Practice acknowledges that children's needs may intersect all the aforementioned areas. For example, we can imagine that a child with foetal alcohol syndrome may have difficulties with communication and interaction, and how they learn, as well as specific physical needs that may need specific curriculum arrangements to support their education. Or perhaps the child is diagnosed with paediatric autoimmune neuropsychiatric disorders (PANDAs) associated with streptococcal infection, which may present via tics, obsessive-compulsive disorder (OCD) and other mental health difficulties. Whilst emanating from a physical need (an infection), the after-effects may be considered within the realms of SEMH. These overlaps may also be argued for many of the other needs discussed in the book as well as others within the series.

The reasoning for broad areas of needs in the SEND Code of Practice is to understand a child's primary needs and what might be the best intervention and support to provide them in the mainstream, or a signpost for specific specialist provision. The difficulty in this is that it is likely that children will have a range of needs that do not necessarily fit in the specific tidy boxes represented earlier, yet services and supports attempt to delineate their provisions accordingly. Moreover, the schooling programme in the UK may offer 'SEMH' schools that offer support for children with externalised behaviours that are seen as disruptive to learning in the mainstream but may not cater for those who may internalise some of their difficulties.

The SEND Code of Practice attempts to define what is meant by SEMH and how it may be expressed within behaviour. These are some of the words used to describe SEMH difficulties Department for Education, Department for Health, 2022, p. 98):

- withdrawn
- isolated
- challenging
- disruptive
- disturbing

The SEND Code of Practice also cites that these behaviours may be reflective of a child's mental health difficulty including:

- anxiety
- depression
- eating disorders

Interestingly, self-harming and substance misuse are noted to be mental health difficulties within themselves rather than being symptomatic of a mental health difficulty. The SEND Code of Practice then goes on to differentiate disorders from mental health difficulties such as:

- attention deficit disorder (ADD)
- attention deficit hyperactivity disorder (ADHD)
- attachment disorder

It is unclear in the document why there is a specific differentiation between mental health difficulties and disorders. Nor is there specific reference that ADHD may affect someone's mood through self-esteem, anxiety or depression. These are some of the considerations that will be discussed in this book to help educators consider their role in supporting children's wellbeing, especially when being identified as having SEMH needs.

In understanding SEMH, Mainstone-Cotton (2021, pp. 26–32) encourages practitioners to be professionally curious about a child's behaviour, their health, how they play and their family history. This approach is less about diagnostic criteria or neurodiversity but rather an understanding of a child within the wider context of a child's life history, their experience and their environments. Mainstone-Cotton (p. 7) further identifies SEMH in three specific areas:

- children who find everyday change difficult and scary
- children who find it hard to develop relationships with adults and/or children
- children who find it hard to participate in activities or routines with others in the group

A BRIEF OVERVIEW OF THE INTERNATIONAL POLICY PICTURE

The education of children is undoubtedly important and as such is enshrined in the United Nations Convention on the Rights of the Child (UNCRC), which is globally ratified by most countries in the world. However, several rights are outlined in the UNCRC and are not just about education or access to it. Within the UNCRC it is asserted that there is no hierarchy of rights and that they should be seen as equal (UNICEF, 2022). The UNCRC includes articles relating to non-discrimination; protection from violence, abuse and neglect; specific rights for children with disabilities; rights to education; and support in recovery from trauma and abuse.

Children with SEMH may be identified as having a disability. The Equality Act (Gov.uk, 2022) asserts that you may be considered disabled under the Equality Act 2010 "if you have a physical or mental impairment that has a 'substantial' and 'long-term' negative effect on your ability to do normal daily activities". It is reasonable to conclude that some of the SEMH needs discussed in this book have a substantial and long-term effect on a child's schooling. Whilst I am not particularly enamoured by the term 'mental impairment' for all the pathologising of neurodiversity and negative connotations of being 'impaired', it does at least help to reiterate how the rights of individual children should be protected.

Education has an important part to play regarding recovery from trauma and abuse, and unsurprisingly those children with SEMH may be exhibiting their experience of neglect and abuse through their behaviour.

As I write this book, I am acutely aware of the war in Ukraine, the girls in Afghanistan denied an education and the SEND crisis in the UK that means thousands of children are without an educational placement. The articles of the UNCRC may be simple to understand but it appears that we have fundamental responsibilities, not just as a global community but even nationally in the UK to make sure we are meeting the needs of all children in our local communities. This book provides a snapshot, a minuscule contribution to the huge task ahead of what it means to include all children within an education system. And I know even as I write this, that upon publication this will be out of date. You will add to this paragraph other national events that have a daily impact on the children that you work and care for.

WHAT DOES IT MEAN TO HAVE SOCIAL, EMOTIONAL AND MENTAL HEALTH NEEDS?

I have explored the wider context to explain some key aspects relating to SEMH, but what does this mean for a teacher who is trying to support their children? Well, we begin to see SEMH as complicated and that there is no one specific approach that may make things simpler within the class. Instead, it is about having a broader understanding of SEMH within the context of your school, your understanding and your own personal approach. To help you with this huge task, I have considered some key aspects of SEMH and some broad unifying features of the term, as well as how this may be displayed within the class and the broader school environment.

The key feature of SEMH is the difficulty that children may have in regulating their emotional state. They may find that their feelings of upset, sadness, anger, frustration or anxiety (and many more besides) are difficult to name and tame. Children may find their emotions, whatever they are, difficult to be able to manage or regulate. Those feelings then externalise and manifest into what we see as behaviour.

These behaviours may become disruptive to the class teacher who may have to focus their attention on one child's needs that are difficult to contain and may require significant resources (in terms of support and planning).

Others may notice that these children may also be highly sensitive to changes in their environment, routines and relationships. Children may be able to contain, mask or hide their emotional state in certain environments – perhaps because they feel worried to express them publicly – but find outlets later on when it is safe to do so. Other children may not be able to do this, and there is little time to filter between their feelings and their actions. For example, if they feel frightened, then they may throw something to keep the perceived danger out of their way. Compare this to the child who may have the same feelings but not outwardly show a response until they get home and have lots of internal worries that they may express by refusing to go to school the following day. Further complicating implementing strategies to support a child in class is not only our limited understanding of why a child may behave in a certain way, but even if we were to ask a child, they may not know themselves.

The following case studies are a way of representing some of these key features of SEMH. None of them go into details around diagnosis, labels or identifying of specific neurodiversity but instead focus on throwing light on what education staff may see in the school environment. The purpose of case studies is to explore your perception and values, and in doing so I encourage you to think about how you might respond to each situation and how you would like to respond. To help this exploration, the case studies are divided into familiar phases of the school day.

CASE STUDY 1: COMING INTO SCHOOL

Pupil A is nine years old and has been attending the school since reception. They have always found it difficult to leave their mum at the school gate and often appear tearful and sometimes refuse to stop hugging their mum, making them late for registration. The mum has reported that the child often cries the night before, refuses to get dressed to come to school, and says that they hate school and don't want to come in. This morning as Pupil A and their mum approach the school gate, Pupil A is crying as their classmates walk past them to file into school. Pupil A is holding on to mum and says that they don't want to come in, they hate school and wish they could stay at home.

CASE STUDY 2: IN THE CLASSROOM

Pupil B is seven years old and has joined the school this year. Initially, Pupil B seemed settled and would start their work without much input. The work was of poor quality, with frequent spelling mistakes, and large unjoined and scrawled handwriting. In the recent few weeks, Pupil B has been reluctant to start their work, and when they do they frequently tear it up and throw it on the floor. There have been occasions when they have been refusing to work at all and instead exit the class without permission and wander into other classrooms. When asked to leave the classroom they would then throw pencils and other resources on the floor.

CASE STUDY 3: IN THE PLAYGROUND

Pupil C is nine years old and has been at the school since year 3. They left their previous school in reception after their parents moved to a larger house. Pupil C has a younger sister at the school. Pupil C rarely plays with other children but did initially try to. However, when playing with other children, Pupil C often gets into physical fights such as pulling hair, spitting at others and biting them. Soon, other children stopped playing with Pupil C. Instead, Pupil C sits by themselves at break time and lunchtime. They have been offered time in the nurture space at break time, but Pupil C says that "it's boring".

CASE STUDY 4: IN THE LUNCH HALL

Pupil D is ten years old and has attended the same primary school since the beginning of compulsory schooling. At first, they ate school 'hot dinners' in the main lunch hall but would only eat the salad that was offered before insisting on only eating beige food. Pupil D would attempt to avoid the dining room and asked their parents to provide packed lunch. With a packed lunch, Pupil D would eat plain pitta with hummus, and crisps. Eventually, Pupil D refused to eat at school at all.

CASE STUDY 5: GOING HOME

Pupil E is nine years old and has a diagnosis of ADHD and is autistic. Throughout the day, they use now and next cards. Pupil E, at the end of the school day, refuses to put on their coat whatever the weather and won't pack up their books to take home. Pupil E will not do reading at home, saying, "Work is for school and home is for rest". Irrespective of how much the teacher tries to reason or encourage Pupil E to wear a coat or to take a reading book home, they won't.

The case studies attempt to minimise the use of demographic details; they could be any pupil: any gender, ethnic background and from any country. Case studies can be helpful to not just explore the nature of the children that it focusses on but also our own nature. Our biases, our thoughts and the values we apply to different behaviours. For example, when you read case study 2 (in the classroom) what words do you associate with the child? Do you think they are naughty or scared? Have low self-esteem or are angry? Are these labels binary or can they co-exist at the same time? Moreover, if you read these case studies and then considered if they had specific diagnoses or profiles, does it mean that you are more inclined to think of punitive punishments or supportive consequences? How we understand the children that we work with is likely to influence how we might aim to support them. The culture of a school becomes incredibly important; the classroom is the microcosm of the larger environment and how the teacher responds to moments in the classroom is likely to be reflected in the wider environment. Beyond that of the school is the community in which we work.

Social, emotional and mental health is heavily connected to child development and several key theorists review development that is relevant to SEMH. I begin by looking at Piaget's work (Ansorge, 2020) which identifies four specific stages of child development, and how children relate and learn through their world environment. Following is a table that provides a brief overview of these stages.

Age	Stage name	What is it?	Learning from
Birth to 2 years	Sensorimotor	Learning the difference between themselves and their external environment.	Sensory experiences and manipulation of objects around them
4-7 years of age	Preoperational	Begin to engage in symbolic play and to understand symbols. For example, using a stick to represent a wand.	Learning through role-play
7-11 years of age	Concrete operational	Children are able to grasp more concrete things but may still struggle with things that are more abstract.	Beginnings of using logic
12 years of age into adulthood	Formal operational	Thinking becomes more sophisticated. Can consider abstract and more complicated ideas.	Logical thought Deductive reasoning Problem solving

These stages are important as they allow educators to under-stand what may be seen as typical behaviour of different-aged children (Asquith, 2020, p. 43). For example, our expectations of a four-year-old are likely to be very different to that of an 11-year-old.

In this book, strategies are provided for the sensorimotor, preoperational and concrete operational stages. As this book is aimed to support children under the age of 12, there is less focus on the formal operational stage (the ability to reason, to problem solve and logical thought) but more scaffolding for this approach instead.

SEMH does not just sit within the development of the child, but also with the interaction between the school, teachers, staff and parents/carers. It is the moments that children share in the playground, the relationships between teacher and pupils in the classroom, and the thoughts and feelings about school long after the school gates close.

In more recent years there has been more focussed discussion on ableist approaches to understanding differences. Ableism refers to the discriminatory understanding of disability from a person/organisation with a non-disabled perspective. We can see this in the context of the schooling community enacted through the restriction and choices being made with those who aren't disabled on behalf of those without power. Those with SEMH needs may be subject to changes and a reduction of their experiences of the school environment through reduced timetables or spaces which they are not allowed to enter but others are. Another way this may be seen is by the refusal to make reasonable adjustments, citing rules as a go-to.

How we understand SEMH is entrenched in the language we use, which may evoke specific views of gender, race, culture or ethnicity. Many of the terms we use or might hear other children call one another may also be ensconced in heteronormative perspectives. Consider some of the following words and how you may envisage the child they could be describing:

Daydreamer
Lazy
Manipulative
Overactive
Weird
Bold
Cry-baby
Inconsiderate
Spiteful
Shy
Feisty
Active
Disruptive Thoughtless
Erratic
Assertive
Sensitive
Bossy
Irrational
Nervous
Fidgety
Naughty
Strange
Neurotic
Anxious
Violent
Aggressive
Talkative
Belligerent
Domineering
Emotional

Then consider, not just what the word says about the child that we are attempting to describe or has been described, but how it reflects on us as professionals. The words that we use are important; they may be a way in which we can prioritise where we focus our resources (for example, we are more likely to provide additional resources for a child who is described as violent compared to naughty), or words can also risk labelling a child in a way which is not helpful for their social development and from an ableist approach. For example, if we are to tell a child that they are brave and not to cry, then are we saying that they should not show their emotions in a public place (Thierry, 2017)? Moreover, are we more likely to encourage certain emotional responses depending on an individual's intersectionality?

I will finish this chapter with some testimonies/quotes from the parents/carers of children about their experiences of SEMH. When you read them consider what aspects you might notice within the schooling environment. Is it always obvious or are there aspects that you would need to find out more about to really understand? How could you as an educational practitioner find out more about the experiences of children and their parents/carers in these situations?

> I would wake up in the morning not knowing what the morning was going to be. I'd go to bed with a feeling of dread. Was there going to be screaming and shouting? Was Lily going to refuse to go to school? It makes me feel like a rubbish mum. A mum that starts the day shouting just as much as Lily does.
> > (From the mum of a child with generalised anxiety disorder)

> I'd get a call from school telling me that my daughter was blocking the classroom door. I'd go to school, and she'd be lying between the classroom door and the corridor. Face down, hitting the floor. Like a toddler. She was nine. They'd be times we would go to the park, and I'd turn round and she'd be jogging with a man that we didn't know and I'd have to call her to come back. She'd sit on people's laps,

people she hardly knew. It was exhausting, always having to watch her as she had no idea about how to try and keep safe.

(From the appointed guardian of a child with disinhibited social engagement disorder)

Patrick always really enjoyed school and had lots of friends as soon as he started. He would love to play with others. But as he went into year two things became harder for him. He hated sitting at the table, he hated story-time, he hated writing. It felt like he hated everything. The teacher told me how he'd constantly be distracted, getting up from his seat, would have to be told what to do again and again. Eventually he started getting into trouble. He'd walk out of class, slam doors, and be sent to the Head Teacher's office or sometimes another teacher's class where he would have to work in silence. He couldn't do it. I took him to the GP and after a long time, a long wait … lots of forms to fill in and back and forth, we were told he had ADHD. It helped knowing he had ADHD as we could start to explain to him what it meant and think of ways to help him instead of telling him off.

(From the dad of a child with ADHD)

Part 2

PRACTICAL
STRATEGIES

PRACTICAL STRATEGIES

This Part focuses on practical strategies that early years practitioners, teachers, support assistants and senior leaders can implement within the context of their schools to include children with a range of needs. The aim is to ensure that education staff feel empowered to think of a range of ways to support children being included and thriving within the early years and school environment. Whilst reading this Part, it is important to recognise that the aim of this guide is not a list of things to 'do' to the child but to have a collaborative discussion with the child and their families.

Returning to the United Nations Convention on the Rights of the Child (UNCRC) and highlighting article 3 (UNICEF, 2022), it details that the "best interests of the child must be a top priority in all decisions and actions that affect children". When we are looking at strategies that may be helpful, we must assign the value that it is in the best interest of the child that we are ultimately trying to support as well as the wider school environment. There is often tension with ideas concerning the best interest of the child and the best interests of the wider group setting. This book uses the lens of article 3 – the best interest of the child – as a lens in which to provide support.

The information in this Part is generally divided in the following way:

- the specific need
- ideas concerning intervention, support and adaptions
- consideration of bridging the gap between home and school

There are some exceptions to this, especially with the information about harmful sexual behaviour as this focusses on risk

DOI: 10.4324/9781003273097-4

assessment and working within a multidisciplinary approach. However, for the most part, an approach that you may wish to use is presenting different ideas to a child and their family and seeing what they think might be helpful. You can then explore different ideas together and see how successful they might be in their implementation. Another way of using this book is to consider a particular child, and then audit what strategies are in place for them already and what might be helpful to implement in the future. Some of the ideas may be things that can be embedded within the wider curriculum and arrangements within the schooling environment.

In view of my previous comments criticising the ableist approach, some people would consider me neurodivergent, as I have Tourette's syndrome. I also have clinical depression, which I take regular medication for, and previously have experienced PTSD and obsessive-compulsive disorder. I have used some of these experiences to 'sense check' what is being written as well as drawing on others' experiences with their express permission. In the instances of SEMH needs that I do not have and have never had, I have asked those to review what I have written, and where they thought it was appropriate, to make changes or expand on certain points. I am also indebted to them for the time they have taken to provide further strategies and ideas that you might find useful in your work.

ANXIETY

Anxiety is the feeling that exists from a threat – perceived or real. Whilst worry or feelings of anxiety may exist prior to a test or at an activity a child doesn't like, the feelings are likely to dissipate. An anxiety disorder, however, has longevity and goes beyond preparing for an event. Anxiety may affect what a child will do or how they respond to situations. A simple approach to understanding anxiety often draws upon ideas of evolutionary psychology – that we have survived as a species because we respond to threats. These threats present a danger to our lives, for example, wild animals, heights, and fire. It is considered that humans have different responses to threats to help protect them. These are freeze (to stay in one place), flight (to run away from the threat) or fight (to physically interact with the threat).

Anxiety disorders are defined in the *Diagnostic and Statistical Manual of Mental Disorders* (5th ed.) as:

> Excessive anxiety and worry (apprehensive expectation), occurring more days than not for at least 6 months, about a number of events or activities (such as work or school performance).
>
> *(American Psychiatric Association, 2013, Table 3.15)*

Furthering this, the American Psychiatric Association also asserts that "the person finds it difficult to control the worry" and goes into detail that at least some of the following six symptoms must also co-occur:

- restlessness
- being easily tired

DOI: 10.4324/9781003273097-5

- difficulty concentrating
- being irritable
- muscle tension
- sleep disturbances
     (American Psychiatric Association, 2013, Table 3.15)

As educators, we can see how issues relating to irritability, concentration and sleep disturbances might have a specific effect on a child's functioning within the school environment.

What is different to a typical reaction to threats or perception of threats in anxiety disorder is how it affects an individual's functioning and the longevity of anxiety with symptoms being noted for at least six months. We can see that anxiety anticipating an upcoming test, waiting to go on a rollercoaster or getting on an aeroplane would likely be as short-lived as the event itself. However, with an anxiety disorder, these feelings extend beyond the event.

The term *anxiety disorder* can be seen as an umbrella term that includes a range of presentations within it. The following sections focus on those which I believe may have the most impact on a younger child's relationship with the schooling environment. These are emotionally based school avoidance, generalised anxiety, social anxiety and specific phobias.

EMOTIONALLY BASED SCHOOL AVOIDANCE

Emotionally based school avoidance (EBSA) has a number of names associated with it. You may have heard EBSA or the behaviours associated with it referred to as:

- school refusal/school refuser
- school phobia/school phobic
- truancy/truant
- persistent absenteeism

The reasons for a child's persistent absence from school are likely to be varied and include a range of factors. It may be worth considering other books in this series such as those relating to speech and language needs and autistic spectrum conditions, which may complicate children's difficulties in attending schools. EBSA is not an anxiety disorder in itself but one which, in some instances, may be partly explained by anxiety but also may be understood in the context of unmet or misunderstood needs, sensory difficulties or depression.

EBSA is a term that is beginning to be used more frequently in the UK and provides a more descriptive understanding than that of 'school refuser', which is seen to problematise the child and assume that the child is making a deliberate decision to not attend school. As partially explained earlier, EBSA is not a diagnosis but an umbrella term which aims to describe groups of children who have severe difficulties in attending school (Thambirajah, De-Hayes, & Grandinson, 2007).

EBSA includes those children who find it difficult to attend school due to underlying difficulties such as anxiety or worries about leaving their parents/carers. These feelings might manifest physically with somatic symptoms (such as headaches or stomach pains) as well as distress (such as crying and non-attendance to school). Those with EBSA are likely to demonstrate their worries the night before. This can also have the further effects of disrupting a child's sleep and increasing feelings of irritability. The child could be increasingly unlikely to be resilient to stresses and challenges within the school environment.

Further to this, different localities will have different responses to EBSA. Some areas may issue fines to parents for non-attendance, some schools might ask parents to bring their child (even in their pyjamas) and others might provide part-time timetables. The nature of EBSA is that it often challenges key performance indicators for a school organisation (i.e. attendance), and this can mean that the focus is getting the child to attend at all costs rather than on the individual child and their well-being.

Typically, in these sections I provide suggestions on what to do if a child presents with a difficulty, but I will make an exception for EBSA and say very clearly what not to do. Do not ask a parent/carer to bring in a child irrespective of the child's emotional state. If the child were an adult, we would be look-ing at approaches to make sure they felt safe and confident in attending school; we certainly wouldn't be insisting that an adult come in to work or go outside in their pyjamas. Forced attendance can cause more difficulty and further isolate a child. Coming to school in pyjamas is likely to marginalise a child and cause them embarrassment. This isn't a way of encouraging long-term attendance to school but only provides a short-term, instant solution to a situation which requires planning and sup-port in a wider way. It is also distressing for both the child and adults in the situation and has the potential to break down issues relating to trust.

The approach to supporting a child's attendance at school is to consider what is driving the EBSA. Is it anxiety? If so, then continue reading through this section and consider approaches that might support the child and their family. Or perhaps it is more akin to sensory difficulties (too noisy, too loud, too bright)? If so, then it might be important to look at strategies where a child has a 'safe space' to which they can take them-selves. Or maybe it is because a child has suffered from a trau-matic experience which requires careful planning to allow them to feel safe to leave a parent and go to school.

Here, it takes professional curiosity to find out what is driv-ing the underlying avoidance of school and what is driving the extreme emotional response.

GENERALISED ANXIETY

Generalised anxiety is an anxiety disorder which is character-ised by the following:

- Excessive anxiety and worry about a range of different top-ics, activities or events.
- This worry is hard to manage and control.
- The worry also is coupled with one of the following:
  - feelings of edginess or restlessness
  - feeling of tiredness
  - difficulty in concentrating

- being irritable
- sore and aching muscles
- finding it hard to sleep (getting to sleep, staying asleep or being satisfied by sleep)

(Very Well Mind, 2022)

As an educational practitioner, you might notice that children with generalised anxiety disorder respond in lots of different ways to feelings of anxiety. A child with generalised anxiety disorders may worry about a range of things "from the past, the present, and the future" (Padmore, 2016). For some children, their anxiety leads to lack of attendance and means that you may not see them at all in your role within school. For others, their anxiety is demonstrated in ways that you might consider more typical of anxiety (e.g. tearfulness, hiding in toilets/under the table), whilst for other children their anxiety is demonstrated by being aggressive and angry towards others. Fear can be expressed in different ways, including anger (Thierry, 2017).

SOCIAL PHOBIA/ANXIETY

Whilst generalised anxiety is non-specific, social anxiety, as the name suggests, is orientated around intense worries around social situations. These social situations provoke feelings of fear or anxiety, and children may show this by crying, having what we see as 'tantrums', they might cling to familiar people or not speak in social situations (American Psychiatric Association, 2013). We can see that in schooling environments, especially situations that may be unfamiliar, the social demands may mean that children find it really difficult to engage in group activities, learning environments or playtime activities.

SPECIFIC PHOBIAS

Specific phobias in children are relatively common, with main phobias present between 4 and 6 years of age, peaking at ages 7–9, and declining again between the ages of 10 and 12 (Kokanovic & Barron, 2021). Phobias emanating in childhood tend to fit within the following areas:

- animals (for example, dogs, birds, spiders, wasps)
- natural environment
- blood, injection or injuries
- situational
- other (such as contracting illness)

Phobias are a fairly typical part of growing up, reflecting children's developing cognitive abilities; and children will usually show fearful reactions to things such as strangers, loud noises, darkness, imaginary creatures such as monsters, and real creatures like snakes and spiders (Ollendick, King, & Miris, 2002). Girls are more likely to exhibit specific phobias than boys. Some phobias may be obvious in your own home life if you have taken a child into a public toilet and they have refused to use the hand dryer for example. The fear may demonstrate itself through avoiding where they may be exposed to the thing of fear (for example walking past certain houses that may have dogs), or they may hide under tables, scream, run away or shout when they see the object that they fear.

SELECTIVE MUTISM/SITUATIONAL MUTISM

Selective mutism is an anxiety disorder which is characterised by a person's inability to speak in certain situations. For children, this may be in the class to their teacher, with their friends in the playground or perhaps with family members with whom they have infrequent contact. Selective mutism normally starts during childhood and for some can endure into adolescence and adulthood. Children with selective mutism may whisper or speak quietly with little or no spontaneous conversations with adults (White, Bond, & Carroll, 2022).

The most recent *Diagnostic and Statistical Manual* has moved selective mutism from the section "disorders of childhood and adolescence" to the section "anxiety disorders" (Holka-Pokorska, Piróg-Balcerzak, & Jarema, 2018). This made some differences in terms of diagnosis in that selective mutism can now be diagnosed within the adult population, but it also reiterates selective mutism as an anxiety disorder. Selective mutism is normally noticed when a child begins to socialise more beyond their immediate family and therefore there are more significant demands on their ability to talk to others beyond parents and main caregivers. In some studies, a very high proportion of children displaying selective mutism (97% of 30 children) were noted to also meet the clinical threshold of social phobia or avoidant disorder (Black & Uhde, 1995). This may be particularly acute in social situations such as when a child is at school or the playground (Padmore, 2016, p. 93). There has been consideration that selective mutism may be linked to a physically traumatic experience, but there seems to be little evidence that this is the case for the majority of children who present with selective mutism. Selective mutism may be a symptom of anxiety rather than a specific anxiety disorder (Black & Uhde, 1995).

Having selective mutism does not just affect the child but also the development of an effective relationship between the school and parents. Therefore, a key component of addressing this is by considering how to effectively liaise and support parents as well as the child who is presenting with selective mutism. A complicating factor in supporting children is that they may be seen as being quiet, shy or in some cases oppositional (White, Bond, & Carroll, 2022). Selective mutism can also limit a child's opportunities to consolidate learning (Williams, Bishop, & Hadwin, 2021) and therefore consideration of how to include children with selective mutism is paramount.

INTERVENTIONS AND SUPPORT FOR CHILDREN WITH ANXIETY

ANXIETY TOOL 1: CHOICE BOARD

Pupils with anxiety may have experiences of feeling edgy or restless, and find it hard to move from one task to another. Like many of the difficulties described in this book, this can be very challenging in a learning environment where there is often a need to be patient, to be resilient to making mistakes and to be seated.

If a child is feeling restless, they may need the opportunity to expend their energy in positive ways. You can consider a choice board for the child to utilise when things are getting too much. The use of a choice board can be prearranged with the child and parent with positive activities to help distract the child from the cause of anxiety.

Go to read in the reading corner	Do some colouring	Have a walk with support

ANXIETY TOOL 2: 5-POINT SCALE

Some children may not recognise when they feel anxious. In these instances, you may need to support a child in recognising the different emotions and the intensity of those emotions. Different approaches to this can include the use of the 5-point scale (Buron & Curtis, 2012). The use of the 5-point scale was originally designed for autistic children, but its use has moved beyond that. The main purpose of the 5-point scale is to help children be able to notice and respond appropriately to their behaviour. The 5-point scale aims to achieve this by teaching social and emotional content in "a concrete, systematic, and non-judging way" (Buron & Curtis, 2012, p. 1). There are several steps required to make a scale:

1. Identify the difficulty and in this instance, we can name this as *anger*.
2. Determine the skill or social concept that needs to be taught. Using anger as a difficulty we can suggest that we would like a child to understand when they are beginning to become angry and how they might use regulation skills to defuse these feelings.

3. Divide the concept into 5 parts (hence the term 5-point scale).
4. Explain how to use the 5-point scale. This may be through a discussion, a story or even a video to explain how to use it.
5. Evaluate the scale before its use to predict how it may be used in real situations
6. Make a scale which a child can carry around with them to refer to as needed.

(Buron & Curtis, 2012, p. 4)

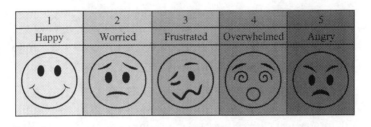

1	2	3	4	5
Happy	Worried	Frustrated	Overwhelmed	Angry

ANXIETY TOOL 3: KEEPING CONTACT WITH FAMILY

If children are tired, they will likely find it difficult to concentrate or, for younger children, even stay awake in class. Feeling tired can also make a child feel irritable and be unfocused.

Having a good relationship with parents/carers is important; keeping a home-school diary might be a way of being able to share information that would be helpful to know. This is referenced later in more detail within interventions for post-traumatic stress disorder. The use of a home-school diary might reveal a range of information. For example, if you know that a child has had a poor night's sleep it could mean that you can put less demand on learning or even provide homework as a follow-up during the weekend. You may wish to consider times in which it is appropriate for a child to come to school later than the normal start day. These times may include when a child has had a poor night's sleep. These discussions and flexibility rely on careful contact and conversations with parents/carers.

ANXIETY TOOL 4: A QUIET SPACE

You may be able to utilise a quiet space for the child to use for low-stimulation activities such as reading or consolidating learning rather than being introduced to new topic areas. This may be a way of them reaffirming their knowledge without 'being at their best' in terms of concentration.

ANXIETY TOOL 5: BREAKING UP LEARNING ACTIVITIES

Finding it difficult to concentrate is counterproductive to the school environment. You might find that a child is unable to focus on a task or is easily distracted from an activity. Some children may experience it feeling like a 'fog' that prevents clarity of thought.

You may wish to break up specific learning activities with simpler tasks that require less concentration. These may be activities such as code breaking, comprehension activities (where the answers are effectively within the resource), colouring or for younger children role-playing, games or reading in the book corner.

ANXIETY TOOL 6: IN AND OUT TRAY

Another approach may include in-tray and out-tray activities so that children can see what is expected of them now and what they have completed. It can mean that if they feel able to, they can pick up where they left off the next day. The in-tray activities can be specific, low-arousal activities (e.g. colouring in, dot-to-dot activities or word searches) that the child has chosen themselves to help reduce anxiety and can be a go-to when they know that they are struggling and finding it hard to concentrate.

ANXIETY TOOL 7: TIME-OUT CARDS

If children are able to decide for themselves, they may be able to use a time-out card to indicate that they are finding it hard to concentrate. This would allow them to communicate with their teacher directly when they need a break from the classroom and go to an alternative space either in or out of the class.

Example 1

TIME-OUT CARD
[child's name] needs a bit of time out of the class. They will go to [designated area] and return after [time or what is decided together].

Example 2

TIME-OUT CARD
I need a time-out for 5 minutes.

ANXIETY TOOL 8: MEETING THE CHILD AT HOME

The inability to speak in certain situations may result in a child using monosyllabic answers (for example yes or no) or providing gestures such as a shake of a head or a nod. They may be able to talk in places that are more familiar to them or where they feel more confident. Often, children feel more confident in home settings. If possible, meeting a child at home can begin to help with their confidence. However, this needs to be sensitively approached, as you don't want to intrude on a child's safe place. This may not always be possible, especially for a class teacher who is likely to have responsibilities for the whole class. Depending on your context and setting, it may be that you can draw upon support from teaching assistants or outreach workers to start developing this programme of support. You might also be able to arrange 'online visits' by utilising virtual meetings to build a child's confidence in knowing who you are and reducing anxiety in this way.

An approach which is less resource driven is that of introducing activities in a place in which a child feels comfortable and confident. For example, does a younger child enjoy a book corner, the library or perhaps a quiet area in the classroom? Finding out by noticing where a child may be more vocal could offer a space in which you can gently introduce topics to a child on a one-to-one basis. For example, imagine that the topic is volcanoes; providing a range of books in the book corner and asking a child to find out three facts about volcanoes that they can write down and give to you may be a way of increasing and developing confidence in a subject area without necessarily relying on their verbal feedback.

ANXIETY TOOL 9: ALTERNATIVES TO SPEAKING

The fear of talking for some children with selective mutism outweighs their fear of disapproval from someone if they do not talk (White, Bond, & Carroll, 2022). This can have implications for children in the classroom environment, for example when asked a direct question from a teacher they may not be able to respond. It can therefore be difficult to correct misunderstandings or check a child's learning.

Choose alternative approaches to verbal responses. The use of mini whiteboards for all children can be a way of allowing everyone to respond to a question without isolating the individual with selective mutism and making them feel different. If resources are an issue, you can ask children to write the answer to a specific question and then you do walk-around checks to identify any misconceptions or strengths in responses. Furthering this, you can ask children to swap the answers with the person next to them and have their classmate read out their answer. This needs to be carefully planned to ensure that the child having their work read out feels happy with this, but also so that it can be a source of pride having their work read out loud for others to hear.

Smaller environments may also allow a child to develop confidence within the classroom setting; this can be achieved through smaller group work or set activities with a partner. Having fewer children in a group may help a child develop confidence in that setting before generalising within the larger setting.

Rewarding children for small achievable goals can help children develop their confidence. These rewards do not need to be external physical awards but can be as simple as a thumbs-up or smiling to help encourage children (Omdal, 2008).

ANXIETY TOOL 10: MOVEMENT BREAKS

Giving children designated breaks may help them refocus after they have become distracted. Depending on the nature of the school, you can ask children to return the registers in the afternoon, or to give out books or pencils. These movement breaks can allow children to take a moment away from the designated task and then refocus when they return to their seats.

SUMMARY

- Anxiety includes different types of presentations (e.g. selective mutism, generalised, emotionally based school avoidance).
- Children present feelings of anxiety differently (fight, flight, freeze).
- Children may not know what they are anxious about or be able to explain it.
- Working with the child/family as well as staff is vital to help develop collaborative approaches.

4

ATTACHMENT AND ATTACHMENT DISORDERS

Attachment is described by Bowlby as the relationships that we have with primary caregivers (Bowlby, 1969, p. 29; Marshall, 2014). Attachments are a key feature of an infant's development, and Bowlby concluded that separation from a primary caregiver can lead to life-long struggles and that the emotional attitude parents show towards their children can have long-term effects on the child (Marshall, 2014, p. 29).

The idea of attachment was furthered by the specific work of Mary Ainsworth, who began with observations of parents and their infants in their homes before designing the experiment the 'strange situation' (Marshall, 2014, p. 29). The strange situation procedure (Ainsworth & Wittig, 1969) details how infants respond differently when their parents leave a room and how they are reassured or not depending on their attachment style.

Most children (and adults) that we know and work with are characterised as having a secure attachment. Their early experiences likely meant they were able to be soothed by a parent, their needs responded to consistently and had the stable presence of a parent. These children are likely (depending on a whole range of other factors discussed within this book!) to be well-adjusted, respond well to teacher input, and be able to be resilient to change and challenges within the schooling environment. In the strange situation, these were the children who were saddened when their primary caregiver left the room but comforted upon their return. However, a number of children responded differently to the same situation, and Ainsworth postulated that they had different attachment styles, namely:

DOI: 10.4324/9781003273097-6

- avoidant attachment
- ambivalent attachment
- disorganised attachment

(Ainsworth & Wittig, 1969)

Marshall argued that several things may affect attachment, these being:

- foetal alcohol spectrum disorder (FASD)
- separation from the birth mother
- multiple home and school moves
- mother having post-natal depression
- premature births
- long-term illness and hospitalisation of the child
- poverty

(Marshall, 2014, p. 29)

It is thought that attachment styles affect the positive internal working model. The positive internal working model refers to a set of expectations and beliefs about the self, others, and the relationship between the self and others. Studies have found that about 60% of children have behaviours which can be secure attachments. Behaviours which may indicate secure attachment include being able to develop friendships, being resilient to changes in the environment and having positive self-esteem. In a typical class of 30 children in the UK, 18 children will have attachments that could be described as secure.

We can see that there are many challenges to developing a secure attachment, and it may depend on the smallest moments between a baby and its primary caregiver. Marshall describes it poetically with the phrase "[it is the] the tiny moments of connection, a look, a smile and touch" (2014, p. 27). However, these small moments can create so much. Bombèr has written extensively on the subject of attachment and education and provides helpful definitions of each (*Inside I'm Hurting*, 2021; and *Know Me to Teach Me*, 2020). In the following table, I have utilised this information to help educators consider how different attachment styles, along with attachment disorders, might present themselves within the classroom and wider school environment. I would like to also take this opportunity to note that attachment styles are not disorders and are not 'diagnosed' or pathological.

		Definition	Causes	Presentation in school and/or class
Attachment style	Secure	What is understood to be the typical attachment style. A child may show some upset when their primary caregiver departs, but they are able to be reassured when they return.	A child's needs are met consistently. The child knows that they can depend on their primary caregiver to support them.	Able to take risks in their learning. Will ask for help if needed.
	Insecure avoidant	Ainsworth identified that the child would explore away from the primary caregiver. If the primary caregiver left the room, the child would not necessarily follow or become upset. Upon the return of the primary caregiver, the child would continue playing without interacting with them.	These homes would be characterised by parents that had little emotional availability or were unresponsive to and even rejected the child. If the child was frustrated or angry, the primary caregiver would still not be forthcoming with their reactions. As a response, the child expressed more anger, frustration and clinginess then those with secure attachment styles.	Fearful or wary of help from others, so may not ask for support. Withdrawal of support from others. Not responding to direct questions (Brooks, 2020, p.140). Not making eye contact (Brooks, 2020, p.140). Children may appear self-sufficient and confident.
	Insecure ambivalent	In the strange situation study, children remained alert to the whereabouts of primary caregivers, even in play, and were upset if caregivers left the room. When the primary caregiver returned, the child would immediately return to them and appear clingy. The child's behaviour upon the caregiver's return would shift between angry outbursts and then being still. Whether the child was angry or non-responsive, they were not soothed by the presence of their caregiver, even if they appeared to be caring and emotionally supportive.	When this attachment style was demonstrated, the primary caregiver was inconsistent in availability; they may be described as preoccupied or not in tune with their children's needs.	Needing attention in classroom environment. Not consoled or comforted by adult support (for example, if they fall over and hurt themselves). Frequent behaviour to gain the attention of the teacher/teaching assistant. Ongoing requests for one-to-one support. Lack of independence in starting or completing tasks.

Disorganised	This type of insecure attachment can present with contradictory and chaotic behaviours. It was found when repeating the strange situation study that some children were characterised as disorganised when their primary caregiver left the room and, upon their return, would go back to their primary caregiver, and then stop and move into the corner.	Uncertain early experiences leading to low self-esteem and poor resilience. Distrust of adults. Not able to tolerate potential humiliation of not knowing a task.	Fearful of adults. Unable to seek support. Refusal to do work or to start engaging in a task (not wishing to fail). They may accuse others in the class of being stupid as a way to deflect from their own fears and worries. May say things like they know it already and therefore it is pointless.
Disorder — Reactive attachment disorder (RAD)	Disorder characterised by being emotionally withdrawn from adults; rarely seeks comfort when distressed.	Experiences of hostile care in the early years. Their primary caregiver was not always a safe adult.	Fearful of adults. Unable to seek support from adults. May show limited emotional responses, so difficult to see the range of emotions.
Disinhibited attachment disorder/disinhibited social engagement disorder (DSED)	Disorder characterised by impulsivity; comfortable with strangers and will happily talk to them without concern or fear of risk.	Experiences of neglect and abandonment, childhood trauma and frequently changing care, such as within placement changes of foster carers or care within orphanages.	Impulsive. May require additional risk assessment with external educational visits.

Whilst I have framed the different attachment styles in neat tidy boxes, we know that humans are more complex than that. Instead, we should take a blended approach to understanding attachment and attachment difficulties. Children (and indeed adults) may have different elements of all styles (Mainstone-Cotton, 2021, p. 22) and require different support at different times.

Next, I discuss in more detail the two specific disorders relating to attachment, namely reactive attachment disorder (RAD) and disinhibited social engagement disorder (DSED).

REACTIVE ATTACHMENT DISORDER (RAD)

Children with RAD exhibit difficulties with having an emotional attachment to their parents/carers. They often behave fearfully with others and have difficulties in managing or expressing their feelings (Seim, Jozefiak, Wichstrøm, Lydersen, & Kayed, 2021). Those diagnosed with RAD are likely to have had an absence of suitable care in the first years of childhood, experienced neglect and abandonment, suffered childhood trauma including sexual abuse, and may have had experiences of foster care or time in orphanages. We can see RAD in children who are likely to have suffered from significant trauma, and it must be caused by social neglect during childhood (American Psychiatric Association, 2013). A child with RAD will have experienced extremely poor care and their emotional needs have not been met; this can have a fundamental effect on their development. Children with RAD may have moved from different caregivers, which prevented them from forming a stable attachment with a trusted adult.

The criteria used to identify RAD in children include:

- a consistent pattern of being emotionally withdrawn toward adult caregivers
- rarely or infrequently seeking comfort when distressed

- rarely responding to comfort when they are distressed
- minimal social and emotional responsiveness to others
- episodes of unexplained irritability, sadness, or fearfulness that are evident even during nonthreatening interactions with adult caregivers.

CASE STUDY 1

Pupil X is five years old and attends their local primary school. Pupil X has been attending school since the beginning of school and has not had any school changes. Pupil X appears to have dealt with transitions well – from coming from class to class and leaving their parent at the gate. When their father drops them off at school, Pupil X walks into school independently. You have never seen Pupil X happy or sad. You have never seen them cry, even when there appear to be friendship difficulties with other children or when they have hurt themselves in the playground. Pupil X will work on their own, but you notice that they often don't understand and won't ask for help. When you ask "Do you need any help?", they just shrug and say "no thank you". In art lessons, they will rarely create anything new but will happily copy the images of their favourite artists.

DISINHIBITED ATTACHMENT DISORDER/DISINHIBITED SOCIAL ENGAGEMENT DISORDER (DSED)

Those children with DSED often appear friendly and outgoing. They are also impulsive, will happily talk to strangers and will not be concerned about leaving with a stranger. These children will have difficulties forming stable and meaningful bonds with others (Seim, Jozefiak, Wichstrøm, Lydersen, & Kayed, 2021).

CASE STUDY 2

Pupil Y is seven years old and attends their local primary school. Pupil Y, whilst having consistently attended their primary school has had several changes in their home lives. They originally lived with their parents but were placed in emergency foster care when they were one and a half years old after the home was found to be abusive and neglectful. Before they were three years old, Pupil Y went to three foster carers before living permanently with their aunt. Pupil Y will happily talk to anyone that comes into the classroom environment and has even attempted to walk home from school on their own without waiting for their aunt. On a visit to a museum, they noticed a man jogging with his dog and attempted to jog with him before they were stopped by a teacher.

INTERVENTION AND SUPPORT FOR CHILDREN WITH REACTIVE ATTACHMENT DISORDER (RAD)

As detailed earlier, a fundamental challenge for children with attachment disorders is being able to establish a safe relationship with adults. Learning that adults are safe and dependable can be a huge task when they have experienced the very opposite, and this has potentially protected them from further harm. Whilst the following ideas may relate to classroom strategies, they must be taken in the context of having an environment which feels safe for a child to be able to take risks in their learning and for that to be celebrated and children not castigated. The physical tools, such as now and next cards, or other approaches in this book will only work if a child is able to learn how to trust, respect and feel supported by the adults around them.

RAD TOOL 1: KEY CONSISTENT ADULT

Being fearful of adults is hugely challenging in school environments, as within the school context there are many adults and relationships that need to be negotiated. Some adults may be known to the child through day-to-day interactions through teaching, the playground and other general touch points in the school day. Other adults may be less familiar to the child and more difficult to build a relationship with, but the child still may have to follow the adults' instructions such as when they are leading an assembly or covering a break time.

However, for a child with RAD, it is helpful to scaffold relationships with the use of a key consistent adult who greets the child at the beginning of the day and debriefs at the end of the day. At the beginning of the day, this may be just a quick hello or something more significant depending on the discussion with the child and their parents/carers. For example, it may be that more significant time is utilised in the morning before lessons start to settle the child; this is sometimes referred to as a 'soft landing'. So rather than simply going straight into class, the child can meet with a key adult to check in with them before doing so. This could be ensuring that a child's basic needs are met: have they eaten, have they left home positively or have there been arguments? Does the child need to settle in terms of requiring co-regulation activities? (Please see Chapter 12, the section titled "Self-regulation" for specific activities that can be incorporated into a meet-and-greet with a consistent adult.) It is likely to be helpful to have an alternative adult available with whom a child can build a relationship.

RAD TOOL 2: VISUAL TIMETABLE

Following is an example of a visual timetable where each topic/subject area can be printed and laminated so that they can be rearranged to match your actual school day. The visual timetable is likely to be set out from top to bottom (depending on cultural references of which ways words are read). As the lesson finishes, you might wish to remove them so children can see what is remaining rather than what has already occurred.

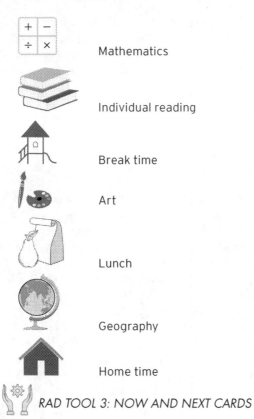

Mathematics

Individual reading

Break time

Art

Lunch

Geography

Home time

RAD TOOL 3: NOW AND NEXT CARDS

Children may be concerned about transitions and changes during the day. The use of visual timetables for the whole class, as described earlier, might be helpful, but you might find that some children would benefit from more specific information that breaks down their day even further. In these cases, the use of now and next cards may help with predictability throughout the school day. A visual timetable is a pictorial representation of the day so that children can quickly see what to expect, whereas now and next cards are broken down in more detail to include what is expected to be done now and what to anticipate later. A typical example of now and next cards is provided next. It is important to make sure that these are regularly updated so that children can refer to them with the knowledge they are accurate. Displaying the broad visual timetable in the morning means that children can then return to this information to check what topics/lessons are being covered. Whilst a visual timetable is useful for larger proportions of the day, if a child requires more personalised support, now and next cards can be used at their table to show what they should be doing immediately (such as reading) and what they can expect to do after that activity.

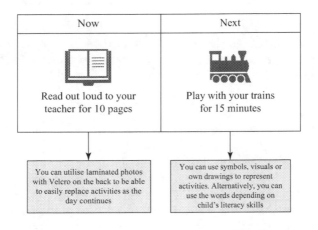

 RAD TOOL 4: USE OF LANGUAGE

As previously highlighted, children with RAD have learned that parents are unsafe, not to be relied on and even dangerous. It is no surprise that seeking support from adults can be seen as a risky endeavour. It may be that you notice that children do not seek clarification or check if they are on the right track with their work.

As a child begins to develop approaches to seek support from adults, you can support the child by checking their understanding, for example, by asking them to reframe the activity or task in their own words. Some examples of different ways of asking questions or commenting on a child's progress are highlighted next:

Instead of	Try
Did you understand?	Can you tell me in your own words what I would like you to do?
Why aren't you working?	I can see that you are thinking. Shall we work this out together?
That's good work.	I really liked the way that you [cite specific activity child achieved]. Can you now [direct task]?

You can also use activities which allow a child to independently sort out correct and incorrect answers. These may be mix-and-match activities so they can work through correct/incorrect answers with minimal adult support.

RAD TOOL 5: ZONES OF REGULATIONS

Children who have developed secure attachment were likely nurtured and cared for in their infant years. Their needs were met, they were soothed when upset and consoled by a reliable adult. On the other hand, children with RAD, when upset, were likely to have been greeted with neglect, inconsistent caregiving and abuse. Their thoughts and feelings were routinely disregarded. These children will have learned that irrespective of their outward emotional response, their needs would not be met. A key aspect of addressing this within the classroom environment is around supporting with co-regulation to help with the later development of self-regulation. (Co-regulation is referred to in more detail in Chapter 12 under the section "Self-regulation".) Other approaches include supporting children with demonstrating their internal world to key adults in their school life.

To help children to recognise their emotions, you may wish to draw upon the use of the 5-point scale discussed in Chapter 3 on anxiety (Buron & Curtis, 2012). Another approach is the use of the zones of regulation (Kuypers, 2011). The zones of regulation is a framework that aims to teach children self-regulation by utilising colours to symbolise states of alertness and emotions (Kuypers, 2011, p. 8). The colours suggested move from blue, which is a low state of alertness, perhaps when a child feels sad or bored; to green, which is a regular state of alertness and can be described as content; to yellow, which is a heightened state of alertness, perhaps when frustrated or excited; to the red zone, which is when there is heightened state of alertness (Kuypers, 2011, p. 9).

The zones of regulation can be used as a specific curriculum to support self-regulation through specific activities. You can also extend this with other approaches, such as the use of wristbands to signify where a child is emotionally within the zones of regulation (or coloured cards on a desk and other such approaches). These can be a signal for grown-ups to intervene and offer alternatives before a child gets to more alert/aroused stages.

INTERVENTION AND SUPPORT FOR CHILDREN WITH DISINHIBITED SOCIAL ENGAGEMENT DISORDER (DSED)

DSED TOOL 1: CALMING ACTIVITIES

Whilst many children may take a moment to decide on want to do next, children with DSED may quickly respond without necessarily thinking of the consequences or the alternatives (Guyon-Harris, et al., 2019). There are several activities suggested in Chapter 5 about attention deficit hyperactivity disorder (ADHD) that may also be helpful to support children who are impulsive. Other approaches that may support a child with DSED include a choice of calming activities as a child enters the classroom. For example, depending on the age of the child you can set up continuous provisions where children have access to self-directed learning and calming activities before more specific teacher-directed work. This could be colouring to encourage mark-making, sorting, organising activities or role-play in small-world environments. The idea is to provide a 'soft landing' for a child to support with emotional regulation and allow them to successfully direct their impulsivity in positive ways within the classroom environment.

DSED TOOL 2: USE OF MINI WHITEBOARDS

If a child is impulsive, they might respond quickly to questions, and you can redirect this energy with the use of mini whiteboards, encouraging the child to write their answers on the whiteboard if they struggle to put their hand up or not call out.

DSED TOOL 3: THE USE OF ROLE-PLAY

The use of role-playing can be helpful in teaching children about personal safety. It is important to create a balance between instilling fear into children and allowing them to effectively risk assess potential dangers and know how to mitigate these risks. This is a very sophisticated skill and one that we learn and develop through our experiences. It is clear that we do not want to put children in risky situations or to worry children, which is why incorporating drawing, colouring, role-playing and stories to help promote discussion around risks without exposing them to the actual difficult situations. For example, you may be able to explore with children some difficulties that may arise if they walk off with a stranger and what might an adult that they know would do in this situation. You can also explore situations within stories by asking children to consider the motivations of characters in the stories.

Some children, despite best intentions, may still be vulnerable to walking off with others. It is therefore important to consider additional risks that may occur when outside of the school environment. For example, during outside events, it may be that you ask for additional adult helpers and ensure that the child is near to the group leader. This adult would need to understand that there are additional risks relating to this child and their potential overfamiliarity with other adults.

DSED TOOL 4: SPECIFIC ROLES IN SCHOOL

Children with DSED may have low self-esteem and not feel like they belong within the school environment. You can look at strategies where children have specific roles within the school. For example, can they give out books at the beginning of the class, take the registers back to the office or show visitors around the school? It is important that although this may be beneficial in some circumstances for the schooling environment, this is with the assumption that due regard has been made to check visitors. It must also be noted that children with DSED may have more difficulty or lack of understanding around risk and this can be exceptionally challenging in open environments. For example, it may be that your playground backs onto a public area or that you are hoping to arrange a school visit to a local museum or gallery where a child's risk within the unfamiliar environment increases.

SUMMARY

Attachment styles or disorders?

- Attachment styles are different from attachment disorders.
- Many children and adults have attachments which are not secure and do not demonstrate behaviour which constitutes a disorder.

Understanding a child's history

- Prior to a child joining a school, it is helpful to visit them at their home or current environment (for example, nursery, pre-school, childcare settings).
- Find out how the child is functioning within those environments and if there are concerns.

Relationships

- Attachment disorders are often played out in the context of relationships.
- Having a safe, dependable adult is vital to support a child's development. They may not have had this in the past. A collaborative approach with parents/carers can support this.
- Supportive transitions are key.

5

ATTENTION DEFICIT HYPERACTIVITY DISORDER (ADHD)

Attention deficit hyperactivity disorder (ADHD) and attention deficit disorder (ADD) first appeared in the *Diagnostic Statistical Manual of Mental Disorders*, 2nd edition in 1968 (American Psychiatric Association, 1968). Just like the term SEMH, ADHD has also had other names. It was originally termed 'hyperkinetic reaction of childhood' before being characterised as a mental disorder in the 1960s by the American Psychiatric Association before the change to the more familiar 'attention deficit disorder with or without hyperactivity'. Now, ADHD is classified within neurodevelopmental disorders, that being a condition which emanates from the development of the brain and how it functions. As such, the key features that form the diagnosis need to be present before the age of 12 years old, so it is particularly pertinent for a book aimed towards teachers of younger children.

ADHD has a number of typifying behaviours, and if a child has at least six symptoms in each of the domains of inattention and hyperactivity, then they may receive a diagnosis of ADHD. These include broad themes of inattention, hyperactivity and impulsivity with specific examples provided in the *Diagnostic Statistical Manual*. This book is not to stand as a rehash of the exact symptoms or as a medical manual, nor is it the role of a teacher to diagnose. Instead, I have chosen some specific areas of difficulty that may help a teacher think about planning, intervention and strategies to include a child.

One important aspect to consider as a teacher is how others view a child with a diagnosis of ADHD as well as the emotional

DOI: 10.4324/9781003273097-7

impact of ADHD on the child. Classroom and school environments are often geared towards the need to concentrate and to
do that for large portions of time, and the relationship between
teacher and pupil can become strained when attempting to 'fit'
a child into the stereotypical ideal classroom environment.

In school alone, a child with ADHD could receive 20,000 cor-
rective or negative comments by the time he or she is 10 years
old (Jellinek, 2010), and it is suggested that children with ADHD
are exposed to significantly more negative comments compared to positive ones. The stigma of ADHD can lead to further
risk associated with a child's dangerousness and well-being and
is further complicated by demographics such as race, ethnicity
and deprivation. There are further considerations on how ADHD
and associated behaviours are perceived by other children and
the potential for children with ADHD to be isolated by others
(Mueller, Tucha, Koerts, & Fuermaier, 2012).

Thus, recognising some of the aspects of ADHD and how it
might affect a child in the school environment is vital, as this
knowledge provides opportunities to consider strategies and
interventions that can better support a child to be included. It is
further vital to reflect on our own views of ADHD and to ensure
that we are professionally curious about what drives behaviour
and to think of strategies to support rather than castigate. In
doing this, I have given examples of some of the behaviours
which are seen as diagnostic criteria and what you may see in
the classroom or school environment.

A key feature in supporting a child with ADHD is making
sure decision-making is fair and transparent. A sense of fair-
ness is important for many children, but perhaps more so for
those with ADHD because they may be less likely to be able to
filter their emotional reaction to feelings of injustice or feelings
of being different and, for some, inferior. It is therefore important to involve children in planning interventions and support,
so they don't feel 'done to' or different from their classmates
without understanding the reason for the intervention. ADHD is
not necessarily the typical idea of a child that can't focus, but

perhaps a better description is a child who struggles to regulate their focus, attention and, for some, emotional reactions.

INTERVENTION AND SUPPORT FOR CHILDREN WITH ADHD

You are likely to find that the difficulties outlined in the following may seem very different depending on the age, stage and context of a child. In the spirit of this book being a helpful companion for educators' work, I have provided different ideas and strategies to support you in including a child who has ADHD. I have drawn from those who have been kind enough to share their experiences of schooling and ADHD, research and literature in the field.

For those children not paying close attention in class, you might notice that a child rushes their schoolwork and finishes before their peers. You might hear phrases such as "I'm done!" from those who wish to verbalise they've completed their work, or other children might get out of their seats, chatting to those around them and distracting others as they feel like they don't have anything to do. Other children might start their work and not realise exactly what the task is, missing out on key things that they should have done. The pupil might not check their work afterwards such as their spelling, punctuation or the other routines of the lesson such as underlining the title or writing the date.

ADHD TOOL 1: USE OF CHECKLISTS

Provide a checklist for the child to complete after they have finished their work. This may help as a prompt for the child when they might not realise that they have not checked their work for mistakes. Remind the pupil that it is okay to make mistakes and that is how we learn! A checklist can be personalised to your expectations as a teacher and the wider school, but the following example might be a helpful starting point.

Have you <u>underlined</u> your work? ☐

Have you put the date on your work? ☐

Are there any spellings that you aren't sure of?
Use a <u>wavy</u> line underneath to tell the teacher
you aren't sure. ☐

Have you used full stops (.)? ☐

Have you used CApiTAl lETters in the right place? ☐

⚙ *ADHD TOOL 2: MINI PERSONAL LESSON PLANS*

As a teacher, you are likely to have a lesson plan (whether or not that is written, or just a clear knowledge of how you expect your lesson to run). In supporting a child in accessing this, knowing what to expect and perhaps being able to follow if there are periods of inattentiveness, a specific mini lesson plan for the child can be helpful.

This lesson plan can allow the child to check through their work and make sure they have not missed anything that you have asked them to do. This may help the pupil who may have become distracted and missed an instruction, so they can refer back to what is on their desk. This can also promote independence rather than feeling like they have to rely on repeatedly asking the teacher.

SAM'S MINI LESSON PLAN

In this lesson we will be finding out about **climate change**.
We will start by **talking to our partner** about what we
    know about climate change.
You will tell me **three facts** about climate change.
We will find out together **two ways** that climate change is
    affecting the earth.
We will write in our books **three ways** we can do something
    different to help reduce the effects of climate change.

ADHD TOOL 3: USE OF FIDGET TOYS

A child might chat to others around them, and this could be seen as being disruptive. They may also get visibly bored in class or drift off from a task and do something else instead. Sometimes a child might get up and wander from their seat. In finding it difficult to focus, you might see that they have incomplete work even though it seems like they understood and had plenty of time to finish. A child that finds it difficult to keep focus may become frustrated, fidgety and want to move. They may also appear to be daydreaming. There are a range of strategies that might support a young person and for them to not feel that they are 'naughty' or disturbing the learning of others.

For those children who are inattentive, fidgeting can be a key approach to support them in staying focussed on their work. You might want to try manipulatives (often called fidget toys) that can keep their hands occupied or a separate piece of paper on which they can doodle. For others they may need specific movement breaks that give them permission to get out of their chair before returning to their work (US Department of Education, 2006).

ADHD TOOL 4: ESTABLISHING CLASSROOM ROUTINES

Due to the other issues highlighted earlier (not paying close attention, difficulty keeping focus), it would come as no surprise that children might not finish their schoolwork. There might be even further distractions in the home environment (think about siblings, pets, computer games, different routines and no set place to complete work) that make it even more challenging to finish homework. The key here is to consider how to help children return to the task at hand to complete their work.

Establish classroom routines that children are used to. This might be that as they enter the classroom they have to collect their books, or they have a particular task in the classroom such as handing out pens. Whatever the routine is make sure that it is consistently applied and that all children are aware of what they are meant to do. It might also help to have visual reminders on the child's desk to help prompt them in case they forget.

Collect your book	Write the date in your book
Make sure you have a pencil	

ADHD TOOL 5: HOME–SCHOOL DIARY

Home-school diaries provide effective communication with parents and opportunities to tick off work the child has completed. An example of a home-school diary is detailed within Chapter 10 on PTSD. A home-school diary may also be connected to a reward chart in agreement and discussion with parents/carers and the child. This should be carefully used so that it is encouraging rather than punitive. Reward charts can be contentious, especially if used to punish rather than reward (for example, taking away a point or moving down from a sunshine to a cloud). Instead, focus on what a child is doing well, and encourage the child to share with a trusted adult when they are doing well and be able to explain why they may have received a reward for a particular piece of work or attitude.

ADHD TOOL 6: USE OF SUPPORT STAFF

Children with ADHD are likely to find it hard to focus. The use of a supportive adult (such as a teaching assistant) to encourage the pupil to refocus on their work can be a helpful approach. To make this worthwhile, there must be opportunities for close preparation between the teacher and support staff. For example, has the teacher made it clear what they intend to be learned in the lesson? Does the teaching assistant have a clear understanding of how they are meant to be supporting the child to be able to access their learning and redirect them? Is the teaching assistant able to identify signs that a child needs a moment away from the work before returning to it? These are all vital aspects in ensuring that the use of support staff is deployed effectively and to meet the needs of the child.

ADHD TOOL 7: CHOICE BOARD

Consider the use of a choice board which has different activities, and the child has to choose one to complete during the lesson, or to provide more structure during break and recreational time. Whilst the choice board is discussed in Chapter 3 on anxiety, where the focus is more on presenting options when a child is dysregulated, the focus here is to support engagement with earlier tasks. A choice board is a graphic organiser that allows a child to visually see what their options are. Depending on what you would like the outcome to be, you might want them to complete all tasks in a set order, do all the tasks but in any order or choose a particular class to complete. An example is given next:

Alexa's choice board	Choose <u>one</u> of the options for breaktime today	
Play a board game in the quiet room	Go to lego club	Play football on the field

ADHD TOOL 8: MOVEMENT BREAKS

Irrespective of a child's age, within the schooling environment there are likely to be expectations that a child will listen to the teacher's instruction. Whilst these may be less obvious during free-flow activities between different types of play, as children get older there is often increased expectation that children sit still, listen and use eye contact to demonstrate to the teacher that they are listening. However, many children might not conform to the neurotypical expectations of some teachers, they may become visibly distracted by looking at other things in the classroom or be absorbed by other activities. It may also be the case that appearing distracted when spoken to may affect peer relationships; if a child doesn't feel they are being listened to or another child talks tangentially it may be that the other person in the conversation feels they are being ignored.

Provide movement breaks for the child so that they can chunk their activities and focus for a shorter amount of time. Consider the use of partner work and how to make sure that each child is effectively communicating. You may wish to use a visual symbol that is a signal for one child to talk and the other to listen. Or it could be that the child with ADHD has a specific task in group or partner work that is structured for them to succeed.

In unstructured times it may be that peer relationships require significant support. In this regard, consider the use of smaller spaces such as nurture rooms where a range of structured activities are provided such as quick, fast-paced board or card games.

ADHD TOOL 9: USE OF CRIB SHEETS

Within the classroom environment, the sequencing of tasks is a key feature in classroom activities. The organisational skills you require before you even get to school include getting dressed, putting shoes on, bringing a water bottle, brushing teeth and so on can be hampered by challenges to sequencing tasks. When a child is at school, this is amplified by being in a space which is not home and needing to be able to get their books, get resources for the lesson, listen to teacher input and then decide on their own output (for example, completing sums, writing paragraphs on a specific subject or making a 3D object). This all requires significant processing of information. This could lead to disorganisation (not having the right things at the right time), not completing work, misunderstanding what needs to be done, doing things out of turn or forgetting what needs to be done in the first place.

Break down tasks into bullet points on a crib sheet, use larger fonts and have a physical gap between sentences. For example:

Rhymes

- On your sheet there are **four** rhymes
- Find the rhymes
- <u>Underline</u> the rhymes

ADHD TOOL 10: ONE-STEP INSTRUCTIONS

Within the class there might be a number of instructions given that a child may struggle to remember and therefore omit without knowing that they have forgotten anything in the first place.

Incorporate the use of one-step instructions. For example, rather than saying "Open your books to page 4 and with your partner identify the adjectives, nouns and verbs in the sentences", break it down to "Open your books to page 4". Wait and scan the room to check that it has been done before issuing the next instruction: "You have five minutes with your partner to identify the adjectives on this page". You can also couple this verbal instruction with a visual timer on your interactive whiteboard, or a physical sand timer so children can see how much time they have left to complete the task. Further, to reiterate these steps, having the instructions physically in front of a child or the wider class might be helpful (adapted from *DSM V*, American Psychiatric Association, 2013).

We can see that the demands of the classroom in particular can be exceedingly challenging for children with ADHD, but with careful planning, support and consideration for children's needs, we can provide an environment where children with ADHD can flourish.

SUMMARY

A question of time

- Timed countdowns (five more minutes, two more minutes)
- Provide visual timers as well as verbal

Focussing

- Break down instructions
- Utilise bullet points for instructions
- Do not just rely on just verbal instruction
- Notebook to write down ideas that come to them
- Permission to get out of their seats
- Choice boards

Sensory overload

- A space to decompress
- Time-out card to signal the need to have some space
- Movement breaks
- Fidget toys

Self-esteem

- Praise
- Recognition when things go well
- Do not punish by taking away the thing that the child is good at
- Opportunities to model turn-taking in structured fun activities

6

FOETAL ALCOHOL SPECTRUM DISORDER (FASD)

Foetal alcohol spectrum disorder (FASD) is a wide and non-clinical diagnosis that describes the physical, cognitive and behavioural effects of prenatal exposure to alcohol (Blackburn, Carpenter, & Egerton, 2012, p. 104). These effects may differ depending on the timing of the alcohol consumption during pregnancy. For example, alcohol may affect the development of facial features if consumed in the first trimester, whilst later alcohol consumption in the third trimester may have specific effects on height, growth and brain development alcohol (Blackburn, Carpenter, & Egerton, 2012, p. 12). FASD often coexists with other conditions such as attention deficit hyperactivity disorder (ADHD), autistic spectrum conditions, oppositional defiance disorder and attachment difficulties (Blackburn, Carpenter, & Egerton, 2012, p. 2).

As this is a book on SEMH, my focus on aspects of FASD are on those which are either characterised as behavioural or that affect children's learning and therefore their interaction within the classroom that can then have a knock-on effect on their emotional well-being and esteem. Whilst I do not linger on some of the physical difficulties that FASD can include (such as facial differences, hearing or visual impairments and so on), these are likely to have an impact on a child's relationship with their learning, and understanding the whole picture is vitally important. The book *Educating Children and Young People with Foetal Alcohol Spectrum Disorders* (Blackburn, Carpenter, & Egerton, 2012) takes a wider view that is likely to be helpful for those teachers who want to have a deeper understanding of the disorder in more detail.

DOI: 10.4324/9781003273097-8

Children with FASD may have difficulties with or exhibit:

- disinhibition
- impulsivity
- inattention
- understanding boundaries
- aggression
- agitation
- planning
- poor concentration
- poor short-term memory
- problem-solving activities
- mathematical concepts
- executive functioning (organisation and planning)
- understanding cause and effect
- speech and language delays and/or disorders

(NHS Ayrshire and Arran, 2022; Blackburn,
Carpenter, & Egerton, 2012)

Moreover, there is evidence that mothers who use alcohol during pregnancy are more likely to smoke and use drugs (Blackburn, Carpenter, & Egerton, 2012, p. 65), further complicating some of the difficulties a child may have with relationships and difficulties within the school environment. It might also be difficult to identify children at risk of FASD, as there may be under-reporting of alcohol use or difficulties in obtaining maternal histories during pregnancy. Children with FASD may also be described as having 'spikey profiles', whereby they may have different developmental areas of strengths and difficulties. For example, it might be that their expressive language is stronger than their physical skills or their comprehension, making it appear as if they understand when in reality they do not (Blackburn, Carpenter, & Egerton, 2012, pp. 64–65; NHS Ayrshire and Arran, 2022, p. 38).

It is important to note that children with FASD may also have additional complicating needs such as difficulties concerning attachment and trauma. I therefore suggest that those chapters of this book are also considered when supporting a child in the class and school environment. It is also key that support is garnered from parents/carers in how best to support their child, as it is likely that difficulties permeate both environments. In 2020, a study by Adoption UK indicated that a quarter of children who are adopted have been affected by alcohol use during pregnancy, as self-reported by the children's current guardians (Grover, 2020). This reiterates that any intervention and support for children with FASD need to take in the holistic view of children's atypical and probably complicated family history.

INTERVENTION AND SUPPORT FOR CHILDREN WITH FASD

As Chapter 5 on ADHD already covers in detail how to support children with impulsivity and inattention, I will not repeat the strategies here and instead recommend that you flip back to that chapter to draw upon ideas there. Instead, here I focus on some of the difficulties that are more specific to FASD and consider how these may affect a child within the schooling environment and strategies that may address some of these difficulties – either to prevent difficulties or to ameliorate challenges. The following intervention and support focus on disinhibition and understanding boundaries, agitation and aggression, and mathematical concepts.

FASD TOOL 1: SOCIAL STORIES

Disinhibition is a wide overarching term which describes how individuals might find it difficult to practice restraint in a social context. It is complicated by children not really understanding their own personal risks and engaging in tasks or activities that other children of the same age may realise are dangerous or could cause harm to them or others. It may also be social conventions such as certain clothing or specific types of touch that are not understood to be problematic in the schooling environment. Examples of this might be a child who hugs a stranger who comes into the classroom or touches their genitalia in public places. Children with FASD may have difficulties with generalising information from one situation to another. They may also have difficulty understanding or misunderstanding complex language (NHS Ayrshire and Arran, 2022, p. 29). In the following interventions, I have borne this in mind to provide ideas that might support a child. However, in the context of children's ability to generalise, you will likely need to adapt and amend the interventions to ensure that the information is concrete and can be directly applied to the situation at hand.

'Social stories' aim to explain why certain behaviours are not appropriate and offer an approach to address specific behaviours. Social stories are sometimes referred to as 'stories that explain' and are a concept initiated by Carol Gray to help children with learning difficulties understand social situations (FASD Toolkit, 2022). A social story is described as a specific resource to develop a child's social skills, especially for those children who are autistic (Gray, "What is a social story", 2022). Gray identifies several key components of a social story:

- describes a context/skill/achievement or concept
- parents/carers must have been part of the discussion
- at least 50% of the content must include praise/achievement of the target audience for the social story
- there must be consideration of who, what, why, when, where and how
- must have an introduction that presents the topic, content that adds detail and a conclusion
- must be of an appropriate length to hold the attention of the target recipient
  (Gray, "It is not a social story if...: A screening tool", 2015)

The primary purpose of social stories is for children with autism. However, there are a number of recommendations to support children with FASD. Social stories for this use are likely to need to be personalised and specific. Understanding when it is appropriate to use a social story requires careful discussion with a child's parents/carers as well as the wider multidisciplinary team. It is also important to acknowledge the specific area of difficulty and behaviour that you want to change. Many social stories use visual tools such as picture exchange communication or cartoons to help a child understand. However, it is important to recognise that children with FASD may find it difficult to generalise from those images (Blackburn, Carpenter, & Egerton, 2012, p. 18) and therefore using photographs of real situations and the child (with the relevant consents in place) means that they are more likely to be able to understand the information that is presented. Consider the following case study:

CASE STUDY: TOUCHING OTHER CHILDREN IN CLASS

Pupil F has FASD and lives with his paternal grandfather. Pupil F is eight years old and they like to hug all the children in the class. Sometimes, they hug visitors to the class, such as inspectors or senior leadership team. However, more recently Pupil F has been hugging another child and kissing them on the cheek. The other pupil doesn't like it. They have told Pupil F to go away and have also pushed them away. Pupil F gets very upset about this and doesn't understand why. Other children in the class have asked Pupil F to leave them alone.

There are several steps to take before the making of a particular social story, as guided by Gray. Using Gray's perspective as a particular focus consider the following questions:

REFLECTIONS

1. Which people would you liaise with?
2. What is the primary behaviour that you want to address?
3. Other than a social story, what other strategies would you use to address this behaviour?

Some vital steps in creating a social story for this young person are:

- To be in contact with the pupil's grandparents.
- To ensure that this behaviour is being addressed across home and school.
- To ensure that the grandparents agree with the social story.
- To ensure that, if the pupil has the capacity, they have helped to co-produce the social story.

Another key factor here is to also use photographs of the child directly in the social story to reaffirm the concrete nature of the instructions that you would like followed in the classroom environment.

Okay ways to touch other people in class ⟶ Use a heading that tells you about the social story

1. I enjoy making friends at school.	2. Sometimes I show my friendship by shaking their hands, giving someone a hug, or kissing their cheek.	3. Not everyone likes to be touched.
4. I want to make sure my friends are happy and feel safe.	5. To help make sure my friends are happy and feel safe I will wave to them in the mornings.	6. If a friend asks me for a hug, I can hug them back if I feel comfortable.

Use photographs of the pupil (with appropriate consent sought)

FASD TOOL 2: SCRIPTING AND DISTRACTION

Children with FASD have permanent brain damage that affects impulse control, social development and emotional immaturity. Aggression within FASD should be seen in this context (NOFASD Australia, 2022), and the responses should support the child in being able to regulate their responses and minimise risk to themselves and others. This may mean that you see children being agitated or aggressive.

Distracting and diverting are helpful techniques for children with FASD (Ory, 2022). You may wish to try using scripts when you can see a child 'bubbling' and finding things difficult. For example, if it was nearing lunchtime you might want to say something like "Lunch is soon, shall we look at the menu together?" or perhaps "What game shall we play at breaktime?" It's important to also utilise the things that the child is interested in. For example, they might like a certain board game, pet or something else that engages their interest. You can also utilise a 'physical prop' (Ory, 2022) when redirecting and distracting a pupil. In the preceding context, you could get out a menu to look at or display the game choices. In other circumstances, you may wish to encourage a walk to a calm space or be given a book to read together. These props may offer a distraction from what was making things difficult for the child in the first place.

FASD TOOL 3: TIME TO PROCESS

Giving time to process information is important. To help, you may wish to give a choice (this can be done visually). Using phrases such as "I can see you are feeling angry, shall we do something else?" and then providing a choice board to support the child diverting as described earlier, but give ample opportunity for this to be a success.

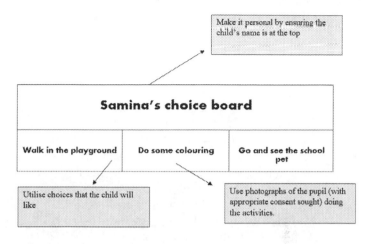

FASD TOOL 4: USE OF LINEAR CLOCKS AND SAND TIMERS

This may seem like a strange inclusion in a book dedicated to supporting children with SEMH needs. However, having difficulties with mathematical concepts can provide significant challenges to concepts of now and next, and to common phrases in the classroom such as "You have five more minutes". Difficulty with mathematical concepts can include challenges with temporal concepts as well as time management (Duke University, 2016). One approach to support children in understanding time is the use of a linear clock. The use of a linear clock is a visual representation of time that relies less on the abstract nature of a clock.

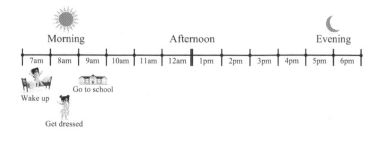

For smaller activities, to denote the time that is remaining, the use of a sand timer provides a visual prompt for children to be able to understand how long they have left for an activity.

FASD TOOL 5: NOW AND NEXT CARDS

Another approach so that a child can see what they are meant to be doing now and what they should be doing next is the use of a now and next board. Although this has been previously mentioned, I am positioning the use of now and next cards with specific adaptions for FASD. To reiterate, now and next boards are simple visual prompts to support a child in recognising what they should be doing at that moment and what they can look forward to or expect afterwards. Typically, these may use visual representations of activities, but as previously discussed, children with FASD may struggle with generalisations, so the use of photographs of the child undertaking the activities may be a slight amendment that would better support them.

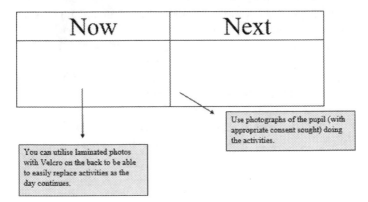

Now	Next

Use photographs of the pupil (with appropriate consent sought) doing the activities.

You can utilise laminated photos with Velcro on the back to be able to easily replace activities as the day continues.

SUMMARY

Remember

- The challenges of a child with FASD emanate from brain development.
- Difficulties with learning can also mean difficulties in social and emotional mental health.

Inclusion

- Promote opportunities for success.
- Keep your language simple.
- Provide one instruction at a time.
- Work with the family to support the child.

7

HARMFUL SEXUAL BEHAVIOUR (HSB)

There is no clear definition of what constitutes harmful sexual behaviour (HSB) (Ey, McInnes, & Rigney, 2017). Nonetheless, broad definitions include developmentally inappropriate sexual behaviour toward either themselves or others (Draugedalen, 2019). This definition relies on people's understanding of what is developmentally typical of a child.

When we talk about children it can be very difficult to talk about how they may exhibit harmful sexual behaviour. There is a range of reasons why this may be, including concerns about labelling a child's behaviour as sexual, not knowing what to do with the information or how to support the child, and acknowledging the child as both a perpetrator and possible victim of sexual abuse. The legislative framework around children that present as having harmful sexual behaviour is outlined in the Children's Act 1989 and furthered with guidance from the Department of Health in the same year (Bateman & Milner, 2015, p. 11).

In this chapter, I am mindful that harmful sexual behaviour may present in a range of settings that will still be concerning for the school environment. For example, there will likely be concerns that behaviour that is demonstrated at home may also pose a risk to other children in the school environment. It is also important to note that whilst some behaviours might happen both in and out of the school environment, interventions within the school may also be supportive of a child (Allardyce & Yates, 2018, p. 86). However, it is important to note that interventions and support for a child displaying harmful sexual behaviour

DOI: 10.4324/9781003273097-9

should be drawn upon from a multidisciplinary approach and not just remain in the hands of teachers and associated support staff. Instead, this chapter should be seen as considerations for a school environment and therefore focuses on how to support pro-social behaviour and effective risk management for both the pupil who displays problematic behaviour and those around them.

I start by offering some examples of what may constitute harmful sexual behaviour.

CASE STUDY 1

Pupil G is a female and ten years old. At break time she chooses to stay in the classroom. In the classroom she undresses and tells others that she is 'having a baby' and masturbates under the table. She asks another child to act as a lookout so that the grown-ups in the school don't know what she is doing. This escalates to her asking one child to watch her 'having a baby' and joining her under the table.

CASE STUDY 2

Pupil H is a male pupil and is nine years old. He brings a mobile phone to school and follows another male pupil into the toilet where he takes pictures of the other child's genitals and threatens the other pupil that he will punch him if he tells an adult about what has happened. The other child is very upset, and it happens on three occasions before he feels able to tell an adult in the school what has happened.

Reading through these case studies consider the following questions:

- How old are the pupils?
- Are there issues around their stage of development that may need to be considered?
- Are there power dynamics that require consideration?
- Where are these events happening?

The other important consideration is not just the child demonstrating HSB, but the victims of the behaviour. Sexual assault or abuse is traumatising for anyone, but within the context of a school it can have further implications on how a child may engage with their learning and is likely to leave emotional scars on a child (Lloyd, 2019). Whilst it is likely that children who perpetuate harmful sexual behaviour are themselves victims, it is vital that those other children targeted by those exhibiting these behaviours are held in mind just as much as those who exhibit such damaging behaviour.

BEYOND REFERRALS

In schools, the dominant process when HSB is identified is that of an individualised response, whereby social care is informed and potentially the police. This response is limited to that individual rather than attempting to disrupt and challenge wider social contexts that may allow for HSB to happen (Lloyd, 2019, p. 3). This can be a challenging task and requires a close understanding of the school and wider community. Unsurprisingly, school leaders and staff should promote a school space in which children can disclose behaviour that they find worrying and that when and if these behaviours are communicated, those children are believed and made safe.

Other aspects concern the culture of the school environment. Are there spaces which are less visible to staff? These are likely to be the spaces which are traditionally 'private' such as toilets or changing rooms. As school leaders, how do we make sure those spaces are made safe as well as maintaining children's privacy? One approach that I use within both the delivery of personal, health and social education (PSHE) and as a parent is the mantra 'there are no secrets, only surprises'. This phrase can be explored in more detail with children – when might a surprise be a happy one? – with the idea that surprises are always revealed, whereas secrets are kept away from others. PSHE is a vital delivery tool to support children in knowing what appropriate touch is, when consent should be sought and what consent looks like in context.

INTERVENTION AND SUPPORT FOR CHILDREN WHO EXHIBIT HSB AND THOSE AROUND THEM

HSB TOOL 1: RISK ASSESSMENT TEMPLATE

The following risk assessment is a combination of various risk assessments that are available online and accessible for use. Many of them draw upon a nationally recognised traffic light system that is a multi-agency tool that colour codes risks and prompts contributors to consider methods to mitigate risk (Brook, 2022). The helpful aspect of this tool is that it reiterates what might be considered typical healthy sexual development and behaviour in context of the child's age and stage of development. The risk assessment encourages a multidisciplinary approach whereby all contribute to the discussion and share information from the different perspectives that they know the child. It then encourages the group to look at strategies to minimise and mitigate risk. As part of this risk assessment, it should be regularly updated and reviewed by a multidisciplinary approach as well as shared with parents/carers and the child about why certain activities are taking place to mitigate risk. I have omitted certain details about the child, as each school and wider community services are likely to have specific information they wish to capture above and beyond a child's age.

RISK MANAGEMENT PLAN

What are the child's strengths?	This is an important aspect to help understand the 'hook' to support a child in engaging in more pro-social behaviour. Are they good at drawing, crafts, computer games? Do they really like maths or can they tell you a myriad of history facts? It is important that when considering risk that there is also balance in helping a child feel like they belong to the wider school community.
What have been the incidents or behaviours that are worrying/ problematic?	What has been noticed or observed? This might be things that have been said, behaviour or things that have been reported. When/if the behaviour was addressed, what was the response by the child or young person? How did parents/carers or wider network respond when the incident was reported?
Are there other behaviour concerns outside of the context of HSB?	For example, has a child been violent, are they disruptive, do they leave class or threaten to hurt other children?
Does the school have specific concerns?	Are there particular children who are being targeted? Are there concerns about others within the family home? Are there aspects around behaviour that need to be discussed to understand wider context?
Who is at risk of harm?	Consider age, group, gender or particular vulnerabilities/ SEND of children that may be targeted.

| Are there any specific locations that are particularly risky? | For example, toilets, particularly quiet or unobserved parts of the playground, changing areas. Consider how this might be managed in terms of additional staffing, opening up/exposing specific spaces. |
| Does the child engage in other risky activities? | The wider context is very important and can help understand how to mitigate risk and further support the child and others around them. Consider, is the child supervised when browsing the internet or using social media? Do they have access to drugs or alcohol? |

HSB TOOL 2: RELEVANT ORGANISATIONS

In working successfully with children with HSB it is vital that we do not only rely on the expertise within the school environment but broaden to other relevant organisations. In the UK, there are a number of long-standing organisations that may be of help, which are referred to at the end of this book in Chapter 13, on further resources. However, please ensure that safeguarding is given due diligence with regard to any organisation that you utilise or draw upon expertise by asking the following questions:

- What are the individual's professional credentials?
- Does the individual have access to clinical supervision?
- Is it mandatory or best practice that they are regulated by a specific healthcare professional association? If yes, are they registered with the appropriate body? In the UK, organisations include:
  - Health and Care Professions Council
  - British Psychological Society
  - General Medical Council

- What are the intended outcomes of engaging with the external agency? For example:
- assessment of need
- individual intervention
- broader understanding of the family context
- development of robust risk assessment

SUMMARY

- There is no specification of what constitutes HSB, but it is understood as inappropriate sexual behaviour relating to age and stage of development.
- Knowing a child's typical development is crucial to understanding what may be atypical and potentially harmful.
- HSB must be addressed through a multidisciplinary approach, with support from agencies outside the schooling environment.

EXTREME/PATHOLOGICAL DEMAND AVOIDANCE (E/PDA)

Pathological demand avoidance (PDA) is understood within the context of autistic spectrum condition (ASC) (Brooks, 2020, p. 30). However, it does not feature as a discrete disorder or condition ratified by either the *Diagnostic and Statistical Manual of Mental Disorders* or the *International Statistical Classification of Diseases and Related Health Problems*. PDA was first described by Elizabeth Newson in the 1980s as a term to describe external behaviours which are characterised by an "extreme resistance to the ordinary demands of everyday life" (Moore, 2020). The term was then validated by the United Kingdom's National Autistic Society as specific behavioural traits that relate to a deficit model of ASC.

PDA is described as a "contested terrain" and this is detailed by Moore (2020). This book is a resource for educators and therefore I will be focussing on how we might understand some of the external behaviours we notice within a school environment and how we can support a child within the context of some of the behaviours described that come under the umbrella of PDA. For some, PDA as a term is contested, as it reiterates the idea of pathological being abnormal. I, therefore, have chosen to use the term extreme demand avoidance (EDA) when considering interventions and support, whilst mindful that much of the literature on the subject refers to it as PDA. EDA can be understood within the context of anxiety, but some strategies may be more useful in supporting children who are understood to have an EDA profile.

DOI: 10.4324/9781003273097-10

Some difficulties that children with EDA have include:

- tolerating everyday pressures and demands
- obsessive behaviour
- impulsivity

(Langton & Frederickson, 2018)

The ways that these behaviours manifest may include:

- using distraction techniques to avoid the task
- attempts to negotiate
- behavioural outbursts

(Langton & Frederickson, 2018)

INTERVENTION AND SUPPORT FOR CHILDREN WITH EDA

If we understand the core difficulties as being driven by a child's anxiety, we can then see the need to support an environment that decreases this anxiety rather than punishing or providing specific consequences for the externalised behaviour. It is likely that a child with EDA also has many difficulties that are exhibited in the home environment as well as at school. Sharing strategies and ways of supporting a child will be vital to ensuring that everyone is supported in the best way possible.

Whilst for many children the use of routines and structure can be supportive, in the case of EDA, this can be counterproductive as these may be seen as demands and something that produces significant anxiety.

EDA TOOL 1: USE INDIRECT LANGUAGE

Children with EDA profiles are likely to refuse direct requests. Instead, the use of indirect language can help with removing the sense of a command. Following are examples that you can incorporate into your teaching, support or conversations at home to support yourself in avoiding the extreme response that comes with what may be conceived as a command.

Instead of	Try
You have ten minutes to clear up.	I wonder if we can find a home for these toys?
Can you do the sums numbered 1–5 please?	I am not sure how to get the answer...?
You need to ...	I am not sure how to do this...
In the next hour, we are going to ...	Maybe we can find out more together...?
Give out the books please.	I wonder if anyone can help me with this?
Can you answer these questions?	I wonder if you can show me how to...?

EDA TOOL 2: DISTRACTION

Distraction can be an effective way of diffusing a situation. Depending on the child's age, stage and interests, you can consider a range of different approaches to reduce a child's anxiety and move away from the source of their worries.

Consider the following case study and think about how you might distract the child before reading the example of how I supported them when they were finding things hard.

CASE STUDY

Pupil I is a female with ASC and with an EDA profile. She is eight years old. She has become very upset in class and has told her teaching assistant that she won't be doing her lesson in the afternoon, which is topic work about space. Instead, she has hidden under the table and is growling from underneath. You know that Pupil I really likes cats.

In this situation, I knew that there were times when this child would get progressively upset. There had been times I had seen that teachers' insistence that she would join in for the session (in this case on space) would mean that she would remain under the table, shout and interrupt the class. Knowing she liked cats I used this as an opportunity to comment on the growling: "Grrrr! Are you a lion or a tiger?" This simple distraction opened up an opportunity to discuss which big cat she was, and then allowed me to say which big cat I was going to be before moving on to find out if cats have ever been in space, because dogs have.

EDA TOOL 3: GIVING CHOICES

Asking a child to put on their shoes may feel quite simple for most, but children with EDA are likely to find this a demand. Instead, give choices so the child feels like they have space to make options. For example, "Do you want to wear your train-ers or shoes today?" Or if you are considering the journey to school, "Do you fancy walking to school today or riding your bike?" In the context of school, you can offer options of where they complete a task or different tasks they can undertake: "Do you want to do this in the quiet area or at the table?"

SUMMARY

- EDA is a profile often associated with ASC; it is not a clinical diagnosis.
- EDA is linked to anxiety and avoidance of situations that provoke or may provoke anxiety.
- EDA can demonstrate itself in behaviour that we may see as challenging and/or oppositional.

SELF-HARM

Self-harm might seem like an odd thing to include in a book concerning children, but we do know that although self-harm is more likely to occur in adolescents, it does occur in younger children. Deliberate self-harm (DSH) is a term to describe a "deliberate act which people engage in with the intention of causing harm to themselves" (Fitzpatrick, 2012, p. 12). Our knowledge of how many children self-harm is limited to presentations to accident and emergency departments and self-reporting within the community (Fitzpatrick, 2012, p. 14). The likelihood is that those children that attend hospital settings are most likely to be self-harming in a way that is most physically serious (i.e., may require medical intervention) or most obvious to a caregiver. It would suggest that there are children who self-harm that do not present within community or hospital settings, and either they hide it from their caregivers so that it isn't known by adults in their lives, or for other reasons it is not recorded.

It is noted that whilst with older children there is a difference in gender representation in hospital and community settings, for those under 12 years old, girls and boys are equally represented (Fitzpatrick, 2012, p. 14).

Self-harm can include:

- ingesting medicines that are available (for example, paracetamol)
- scratching or cutting of skin
- pulling out of hair (trichotillomania)
- picking at the skin (dermatillomania)

There may be other reasons for some of these injuries, and if there are concerns about a child's behaviour and emotional

DOI: 10.4324/9781003273097-11

state, then further external support must be drawn upon. For example, some of these instances I have given of self-harm may be related to obsessive-compulsive disorder or habitual behaviour. It may be that external support from a psychologist, psychiatrist or paediatrician working with the child could reveal more about the reasons behind the behaviour. However, for the purposes of this book, you have signposted appropriately, and you have been informed that the behaviour that you see is that of deliberate self-harm.

Supporting teachers to feel confident in supporting children who self-harm is important. Often teachers have the desire to support but also want to balance the relationship between teacher and child (Fitzpatrick, 2012, p. 89).

Some of the reasons for deliberate self-harm may include:

- to alleviate feelings of being overwhelmed
- to feel something
- to show others how bad they feel
- to punish themselves

(Fitzpatrick, 2012, p. 16)

In the context of the school environment, it may be hard to manage some of these challenges and I would echo the re-occurring thread of this book: seek support from those around you. This support could be directly for the child, such as child and adolescent mental health services, parents/carers or community organisations that may help a child's self-esteem, or the support could be for yourself as well. If your school offers supervision, then this can be used to support your own well-being in addition to drawing upon the expertise of the appropriate safeguarding and senior leadership teams.

SELF-HARM TOOL 1: MOOD DIARY

A mood diary can be used to let children track how they are feeling as well as share it with others who may need to know more about their internal world. This can be especially helpful in circumstances when a child might not publicly say how they feel or use universal tools such as a class mood board, but is more private in nature. The mood diary can be a simple exercise book where children write how they feel, or provide a symbol that expresses their main emotion or an agreed-upon scoring system.

SELF-HARM TOOL 2: DISTRACTION

It may be that the child is able to be distracted from self-harming. This can be through the use of fidget toys, especially for those who need something to occupy their hands when doing classwork. There is limited evidence on how effective distraction is and therefore I recommend talking closely with the child and their parents/carers to see if it is helpful for their particular circumstances. Some children find that distraction through learning a skill, such as crochet or knitting, can be a way of developing their own self-esteem as well as making sure they are physically occupied.

SELF-HARM TOOL 3: VISUAL
COMMUNICATION WITH STAFF

Children who self-harm may find it hard to be able to say to staff how they feel or what they are doing. They might hide what they are doing under the table, or, for some, it might become part of their daily habits that they may not realise. However, for those who do realise, having a visual symbol that lets you know things are difficult for them can be an effective way of them telling you without using their words. Some children like to use a different colour wristband that offers insight into their emotional well-being or a colour card on their table. It might be that you use a traffic light system where green symbolises that everything is okay, amber where things might be 'bubbling' for them, and red indicates that they are really upset or worried. You can abandon the use of a traffic light system altogether and come to a pre-determined use of colours that tell you that things are difficult or use the 5-point scale, as detailed elsewhere in this book.

SELF-HARM TOOL 4: CONVERSATION PROMPTS

Talking about self-harm can be very difficult. It is an evocative subject and can be upsetting for all involved, not just the child who is self-harming. Some feelings include guilt, shame, anger and sadness. It is no wonder that recognising a child who self-harms and then talking about it in a way that doesn't reaffirm those feelings can be difficult. Conversation prompts can help open up conversation whilst not shaming a child and reiterating safeguarding responsibilities.

- "If I am worried about you. I can't keep what you tell me a secret and may have to tell other people to keep you safe."
- "Thank you for telling me about this; it must have been really hard. One of my important jobs, as well as teaching you, is to keep you safe. It might be hard to tell your mum or dad about this, but can we do it together with Mr Smith?"
- "Is there anything we can do to help you feel safe?"
- "Is there anything happening that makes things hard for you?"

The preceding conversation prompts are examples which do not take into account your own style of communication, your knowledge of a child or other factors. They should therefore be amended taking these factors into consideration, with the intent of an open conversation and active listening.

SUMMARY

Individual reasons

- Children may self-harm for different reasons.
- Establishing some of the reasons or patterns can support ways of approaching the behaviour.
- Ensure that school is a safe place and that there are clear structures and strategies in place in cases of bullying or children being left out of play and social groups.

Partnerships with home

- Self-harm can be distressing for not just the child but also parents/carers as well as siblings, friends and other adults in a child's life.
- Developing relationships within the home environment, including regular check-ins, is important.

Working with others

- Talking about self-harm is delicate and not all staff feel confident about it; ensure you engage with child protection/safeguarding staff and seek help for your own emotional well-being.

POST-TRAUMATIC STRESS DISORDER (PTSD)

Post-traumatic stress disorder (PTSD) is a mental health diffi-culty that may follow a traumatic event, either for those that have directly experienced it or for those that have witnessed it. Symptoms may include:

- reliving the event (for example reoccurring memories, nightmares)
- a change in a person's emotional state, such as increased aggression, recklessness or being hypervigilant
- avoiding situations that may bring about difficult memories or thoughts about the events
- negative changes in thoughts and feelings (for example, negative beliefs, feeling alienated and being less interested in life)

(American Psychiatric Association, 2013)

For children under the age of six, there are variations in the symptoms: a lower threshold to diagnose PTSD, along with an increased emphasis on PTSD being a potential conse-quence of witnessing events of others (Tedeschi & Billick, 2017). Additionally, children under the age of six years old do not need to show immediate distress after the event, with the understanding that some children may not be able to verbalise or articulate their emotions (Scheeringa, 2022). Further, some of the diagnostic criteria may be less obvious in children and

DOI: 10.4324/9781003273097-12

therefore internalised and difficult to observe or for younger children to articulate (Tedeschi & Dillick, 2017; Scheeringa, 2022).

Whilst PTSD for some children may be closely related to issues of attachment and trauma, PTSD may also be experienced by children who are witness to terror attacks, displaced by war and conflict, or otherwise may have been exposed to traumatic events inside and outside of the home.

INTERVENTION AND SUPPORT FOR CHILDREN WITH PTSD

PTSD can be complex and affect a child's attendance in school. For some children, school is the environment which provides stability even when other things seem chaotic.

PTSD TOOL 1: USE OF A HOME–SCHOOL DIARY

For children reliving a traumatic event, you might see this re-enacting in play or their drawings. You might also notice that they seem tired, as they have had a poor night's sleep, difficulty dropping off to sleep or waking up in the middle of the night. Some children may also avoid going on overnight school trips, as they might wet the bed.

A challenge in supporting a child in this regard is that their symptoms will often show in the home environment, and you may not know about them. To support children, you are likely to need to know that they are having trouble sleeping, and you may be privy to knowing that they have a diagnosis of PTSD depending on your role within the school and relationships with parents/carers. One approach is to keep a home–school diary that details this helpful information. It does not need to rely on significant amounts of information, but just a quick check-list that helps inform you on whether the child has had a good night's sleep. If the child is able, they can self-report their tiredness or how well they slept.

	How well did you sleep? 1 = ☹ No sleep or interrupted lots and I feel very tired 2 = ☺ My sleep wasn't good or bad, I feel okay 3 = ☺ Amazing sleep, I feel very rested	Any other comments
Monday		
Tuesday		
Wednesday		
Thursday		
Friday		
Tuesday		

PTSD TOOL 2: RESPONDING TO HOME–SCHOOL DIARY

The next step in receiving this information is to respond accordingly. Routines may be very important for a child, and even if they have had a very poor night's sleep, it may be in their best interests to attend school. This is a conversation that can be had with their parents/carers about what is best in instances of very poor sleep. It may be that you can offer a quiet space for a child to rest if they are feeling particularly tired, or make allowances for a child feeling frustrated and finding it difficult to concentrate.

In this instance you might notice that a child is quick-tempered; they might shout at others, they might throw things or otherwise respond in ways that they didn't prior to the traumatic event. They might also find it difficult to settle in class and be distracted, as they are focussing on external events other than their actual learning. Some children may also engage in more risky behaviour such as climbing furniture or attempting to leave school property. Interventions and support for children in managing emotions can be referred to as a tool to support.

PTSD TOOL 3: WALK-THROUGHS OF ENVIRONMENTS

Children may refuse to go past certain places where an event took place; they might find it difficult to go home after school or perhaps to attend school if that is where the traumatic event took place. They may refuse to leave their home, as that could be their safe space. They may not be able to attend or visit new places, as they don't know what to expect and can't control their environment. You can use different approaches to support a child and their family in this regard. One approach is a video walk-through of the environment that you would like the child to attend. This can be simply taken on a mobile phone and emailed to parents/carers (with due regard to safeguarding and data protection relating to the use of e-mails and recordings). A walk-through can include where a child might be expected to enter a building, where key areas are such as toilets and classrooms, as well as places they could go to if they are feeling worried or unsafe.

PTSD TOOL 4: PROVIDE OPPORTUNITIES FOR PLAY

You might notice that a child says that they feel sad, or they might express that they are 'stupid' or talk about the world being a bad place. A child might avoid being around others and stop doing the things that they enjoy. Play can be an important space where children are allowed free expression and it helps develop secure attachment relationships (Whitters, 2021, p. 61). An important component to support children with PTSD is to allow varied opportunities for different types of play, for example, parallel, solitary and co-operative play. Parallel play refers to play when children may play in close proximity to one another but without direct interaction, whilst solitary play is children playing on their own and co-operative play refers to situations when children will play together with a shared goal. Providing opportunities for all three types of play whilst sitting alongside a child and exploring different ways of playing can help pique their interest and engagement.

SUMMARY

- There is a lower threshold for children to receive a diagnosis of PTSD.
- PTSD is a distinct diagnosis beyond that of experiencing traumatic events; not everyone that has experienced trauma will develop PTSD.
- PTSD can affect a range of domains in a child's life.
- Children with PTSD may demonstrate avoidance, intense fear, significant anger and be less interested in normal activities.
- The role of the school is to attempt to provide a safe place for a child to be able to learn.

TIC DISORDERS

TOURETTE'S SYNDROME

Tourette's syndrome is a neurological disorder characterised by motor and vocal tics that wax and wane (change, increase, become less). Tourette's syndrome is named after Gilles de la Tourette, a French doctor who noticed similarities between patients. Tourette's is noted to have a premonitory urge, that is, the feeling that a tic is about to occur before it does. Children may find it difficult to recognise that feeling before it happens. They may also find it uncomfortable, even painful to stop a tic before it happens. Motor tics can include but are not limited to:

- clearing the throat
- hitting different body parts
- blinking
- wincing
- spitting
- rolling the eyes

Motor tics may also appear more complex in nature and have stages, for example:

- touching and licking things
- throwing objects
- banging head against the wall
- falling to the floor

DOI: 10.4324/9781003273097-13

Vocal tics can include:

- grunting
- squeaking
- shouting

Again, similar to motor tics, verbal tics may also sound more complex by including phrases or strings of words:

- swearing or offensive phrases (coprolalia)
- repeating the words of others
- repeating own sounds (echolalia)
- making animal sounds such as barking or purring
- whistling

Interestingly, vocal tics are often categorised into subtypes as indicated by the words in brackets. It is important to note that tics often have several comorbidities, that is, other difficulties or neurodiversities exist alongside the tics. Some examples of these include obsessive-compulsive disorder (OCD), attention deficit hyperactivity disorder (ADHD), and autism spectrum condition (ASC). Tics within the realm of Tourette's syndrome wax and wane; a tic that might be there one day, might not be there the next. Sometimes, certain environments may mean that a child's tics increase, or even mood can have an impact on the number of tics.

PAEDIATRIC AUTOIMMUNE NEUROPSYCHIATRIC DISORDERS ASSOCIATED WITH STREPTOCOCCAL INFECTIONS (PANDAS) AND PAEDIATRIC ACUTE-ONSET NEUROPSYCHIATRIC SYNDROME (PANS)

Paediatric autoimmune neuropsychiatric disorders associated with streptococcal infections (PANDAS) refers to a cluster of symptoms that occurs after children have a streptococcal infection. Streptococcal infection is caused by specific types of bacteria. Most children diagnosed with PANDAS show symptoms before puberty, hence this specific relevance for a book aimed towards younger children (National Institute of Mental Health, 2022). The onset of symptoms of PANDAS is rapid after an infection and these symptoms are predominately OCD and tics. Children might also show intense anxiety about being separated from their parents or other significant people in their lives, and show irritability or variable moods.

PANS on the other hand acknowledges that the child may not have had a streptococcal infection before the onset of neuropsychiatric symptoms. Neither PANDAS and PANS is a diagnosis that features in the *Diagnostic and Statistical Manual of Mental Disorders*, but they are now referred to within the *International Statistical Classification of Diseases* (World Health Organization, 2022).

However, further complicating the search for a diagnosis is that the information provided does not include any specific diagnostic criteria. PANDAS, as a specific disorder, was first described in 1998 by Dr Susan Swedo in which she outlines the specific symptoms of:

- The abrupt and dramatic onset or re-occurrence of obsessive-compulsive disorder (OCD)
- Two additional neuropsychiatric symptoms such as:
    - Anxiety
    - Regression in behaviour
    - Depression
    - Frequent need to urinate
    - Disturbances in sleep
    - Frequent and exaggerated changes in mood (emotional lability)
    - Sensory or motor abnormalities

(Gothenburg University, 2020)

Diagnosis is based on the symptoms and presentation of the above rather than evidence of an autoimmune response.

INTERVENTION, SUPPORT AND
ADAPTATIONS FOR TIC DISORDERS

There are a range of different ways that a school might support a child with tics to be included in school life. As with any chapter in this book, the consideration of strategies should be done in discussion and jointly with the child and their families. They are the ones who are experiencing the tics and will have the best understanding of what things are particularly challenging for them. Whilst the reasons behind a tic disorder such as Tourette's syndrome or PANDAS may be different, the intervention, support and adaptations a school can implement to support a child can be the same. A difference you might wish to consider is the variability of onset.

Whereas a tic disorder may have overlaps with other neurodiversities and potentially genetic predisposition, PANDAS is likely to be more of a dramatic change for the child, their family and the schooling community. Additionally, you are likely to wish to draw upon other chapters in this book, especially that on anxiety (Chapter 3).

It is vital to not punish or attempt to stop physical tics (unless the child risks significant harm to themselves or others). It is key to ensure that other children and adults understand that vocal tics are not intentional, and whilst they may be contextual in nature, they are not intentional and therefore should not be treated as such.

In thinking about adjustments for children with tics, we can consider opportunities throughout the school day to support them. I have divided this section into before school, during school and after school to help practitioners consider the different parts of the days and things that can be done to support children in being included in school life.

TIC DISORDERS TOOL 1: THINKING ABOUT
THE COMPLEXITIES OF JOURNEYS

Some children with Tourette's syndrome and PANS/PANDAS also feature comorbidities such as OCD. These may present by certain compulsions and rituals that require completion. This can have an impact on a child's attendance at school with the potential of children being late as the typical routines of getting ready for school are interrupted. It is reasonable to consider how this is recorded and how you might support a child not feeling additional anxiety about being late to school. It is also helpful to explore with the child and family directly what is affecting lateness and whether or not you can work together to support better punctuality.

Younger children are likely to be supervised on their way to and from school, but being aware of the use of public transport can help children. Some children with Tourette's syndrome and PANDAS/PANS might have more difficulties with sensory processing, and those experiences might make it more difficult to regulate their emotional state. Also, it can be tiring to tic or, conversely, to suppress tics. Be aware that as a child comes into school they may need to decompress and take a moment before getting into the hustle and bustle of school life.

Additionally, on the way to school, children are likely to come across others who may not understand Tourette's syndrome. This may increase children feeling worried about how others might react to their motor or vocal tics. It may be helpful to contact other schools in the area to further educate them about Tourette's syndrome. This would require careful planning and appropriate permission from the child and family to do this.

TIC DISORDERS TOOL 2: OPPORTUNITIES TO TIC

Feeling the need to suppress tics can feel uncomfortable and can be tiring. Some individuals do not want to suppress their tics and/or are unable to. The use of a time-out card or an exit slip would allow the pupil to tic in private and then return to concentrate in class. However, children should not feel pressured to leave the class; rather, it should be an option made available to them should they wish to take it.

In relation to this, careful seating plans can support children to feel that they can leave the class discretely without interrupting the class delivery. This is most likely to be at the back of the class or to the side, but again this requires conversations with the child and family to ensure that this is explained and they agree with the decision-making.

TIC DISORDERS TOOL 3: HELPING WITH THE PAIN OF MOTOR TICS

Motor tics can hurt a child. They may hit their legs, arms and other parts of their body. One approach to ensure children are not in pain is by the use of equipment. For example, a cushion on a child's lap can prevent bruising or pain from motor tics, or a rubber grip at the end of a pencil can be used for the child to chew on rather than biting down on their tongue or grinding their teeth.

SUMMARY

- Tics are likely to change over time.
- The intensity of tics changes; there may be days that feel more settled than others.
- Provide the child and parents/carers opportunities to tell you what they would find helpful.
- Do not punish or give consequences for tics; they are involuntary and should be treated as such.
- The interventions outlined are not to change the course of the tics but to provide opportunities for a child to feel safe in the school environment.

12

MANAGING EMOTIONS

Emotions are the thoughts and feelings that we have as individuals. We may describe them as feelings or mental states, and then define them in more detail with words such as sad, angry, upset, frustrated, happy, content and excited. When an infant is born, we may notice that they show interest (turn towards a sound, for example) or hunger (crying for milk and being settled on the breast or bottle), and from two to four months they may smile spontaneously. Around this time they may also demonstrate surprise or discomfort (I want my nappy changed) as well as laughter. Babies demonstrate these emotions through their facial expressions, the sounds they make and their body movements.

Much of this book is given over to specific diagnoses (for example, ADHD and foetal alcohol spectrum disorder) or profiles (such as extreme/pathological demand avoidance). There are many overlaps between these, and attempts have been made to stress the interconnectedness between different aspects of SEMH. This section explores how children manage their emotions and how this may impact on school life.

SELF-SOOTHING

Self-soothing is an important life skill that helps with a range of areas in a person's life: their sleep, how they manage their feelings, and how they can develop and sustain healthy relationships. Self-soothing is learned when we know how to be soothed by a caregiver as well as external activities (for example, sucking a thumb). Learning how to be calm and to calm is a process that develops through the new experiences that we have (What Is Self-Soothing? Learn About this Important Social-Emotional

DOI: 10.4324/9781003273097-14

Tool", 2022). Self-soothing and self-regulation are closely linked as being able to soothe ourselves when we feel hungry, frustrated, tired and angry and helps us regulate our emotions. Originally, self-soothing emanated as a research term to describe babies who fell back asleep without crying (Hoffman, 2019). Self-soothing is also used to describe those children that sought out the attention of adults to relieve their stress (Hoffman, 2019). For infants, self-soothing can be described as different activities including hugging, putting on music, bathing, massage, the use of a dummy (pacifier), swaddling and shushing (Özurk Dönmez & Bayik Temel, 2019).

Self-soothing is important in the context of schooling, as it allows children to respond effectively to emotions such as embarrassment or feelings of rejection (Lovino, Koslouski, & Chafouleas, 2021). Self-soothing is closely connected to the central nervous system so that any strategies to help a child self-soothe are linked to helping slow down a child's breathing and relaxing their muscles (Lovino, Koslouski, & Chafouleas, 2021). Self-soothing activities that can be utilised are outlined in Chapter 11.

SELF-REGULATION

Self-regulation refers to the ways in which we develop skills to be able to recognise and control our emotions and outward behaviour depending on our contexts (Asquith, 2020, p. 13). Developed by Bandura within social cognitive learning theory, it describes the ability to manage everyday activities such as attention to tasks, developing relationships with others and being able to function effectively within everyday society (Özurk Dönmez & Bayik Temel, 2019).

Self-regulation is developmental and is characterised as evolving throughout childhood. For many of us, we carry the skills of self-regulation into adulthood. For example, for most of us, most of the time, we are likely to be able to keep in check our feelings of frustration, anger and sadness to be able to undertake a range of activities. We may have moments where that becomes more difficult, for example, if experiencing stress in our lives we might find that we are more likely to get cross at another driver on the road who we perceive as driving poorly or find that we are quicker to shout when we don't feel listened to. Skills of self-regulation are changeable depending on other stresses in our lives and more so with children who are still developing these skills.

We can see that self-regulation within the schooling environment is a specific skill that if well-developed can allow children to be able to access their learning effectively, and make and sustain friendships. You may have heard the terms 'dysregulation' or 'dysregulated'; they refer to when an individual doesn't yet have the skills of self-regulation and that lack of regulation may present itself in behaviours such as shouting, throwing items, getting cross and snatching items from others. Bombèr describes dysregulation as "a lack of regulation over basic functions such as arousal levels of feelings" (2021, p. 296).

There are several reasons that children may find it difficult to self-regulate. For example, difficulties with sensory input, challenges with attachment, feelings of anxiety and worries that become overwhelming. Further, a child's ability to use expressive language, the presence of adults to model appropriate behaviour, and the impact of internal and external stimuli can all affect children's (and adults') ability to control their feelings.

Self-regulation in a complicated world can be challenging. As Cowley (2021) poetically states: "as we grow and develop, we must make our way through a world that is frequently puzzling, challenging and difficult to navigate, although one that is often full of joy, wonder and warmth".

These conditions of challenge, puzzle, joy, wonder and warmth are all things that infants, children and adults need to contend with to make sense of the world, and their emotions and the ability to control them have a huge part to play.

Before children can self-regulate, they must be able to co-regulate. Co-regulation is seen as necessary to help children be able to "recognise and identify their feelings" (Asquith, 2020, p. 34). Co-regulation can be supported through careful stages, which are well discussed by Bombèr (2021, p. 205) in her discussion about attachment. Whereas Bombèr characterises the stages as linear in process, I prefer to characterise them as more in a jumble – that being that children may flick between different stages and require different levels of support depending on several factors. These may be in relation to what is happening around children (sensory arousal) as well as internal stimuli (heightened feelings of anxiety). Children may dip in and out of different stages, and as adults, it is important to ensure that we are meeting children where they are so that we are effectively able to support the journey towards co-regulation and self-regulation. This approach is advocated by those who see the adult as a champion in supporting a child to help a child to develop those key skills (Cowley, 2021, p. 67).

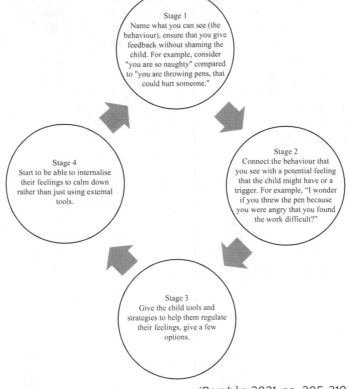

Stage 1
Name what you can see (the behaviour), ensure that you give feedback without shaming the child. For example, consider "you are so naughty" compared to "you are throwing pens, that could hurt someone."

Stage 2
Connect the behaviour that you see with a potential feeling that the child might have or a trigger. For example, "I wonder if you threw the pen because you were angry that you found the work difficult?"

Stage 3
Give the child tools and strategies to help them regulate their feelings, give a few options.

Stage 4
Start to be able to internalise their feelings to calm down rather than just using external tools.

(Bombèr, 2021, pp. 205-210)

For each stage, Bombèr provides different examples of intervention. Rather than rehashing these examples, I have provided case studies of different stages of interaction to help illustrate the different strategies that may be utilised.

CASE STUDY 1

Pupil J is four years old. They have arrived at school and appear unsettled. They didn't want to leave their parent at the school gate and cried for 20 minutes. They refused to take their coat off and shouted at the teacher when asked, saying "go away". Their reception teacher comforts them, bends down so they are at the same level and says, "I think you are feeling sad because you want to see your mummy".

CASE STUDY 2

Pupil K is six years old and complaining they are too hot and their trousers feel uncomfortable. The pupil sits on their own in the playground and shouts at anyone that comes near them. The midday supervisor approaches the pupil and comments, "I think you are angry and that is why you are shouting".

CASE STUDY 3

Pupil L is eight years old and is under a special guardianship order, which means that they live with their grandmother, as their parents were unable to look after them. Their parents were neglectful and there was a history of domestic violence within the family home. Pupil L is blocking the entrance of the classroom by lying in front of the door and screaming. The pupil has a mentor who comes in to support them. They sit on the floor with the child and asks them, "You seem very upset and I think that is why you are lying on the floor. Shall we try doing deep breaths together or perhaps a walk in the playground?"

CASE STUDY 4

Pupil M is ten years old. They feel angry because they were playing football at lunchtime. A child tackled them and hurt their ankles. Pupil M realises they are really angry and notices that they feel 'hot inside' and their face feels flushed. Pupil M leaves the playground and goes to the toilets to sit and calm down. They count to ten and take deep breaths. It takes them a little while, but eventually, they feel less hot and bothered and return to play.

THINKING POINTS

- Do some of the children you work with or know use these approaches to self-regulate?
- Are they always able to use these approaches or is it sometimes more difficult than others?
- For each case study, can you consider what might be the next steps in supporting the child in developing self-regulation skills?
- Would you offer anything alternative to support the children?

Within the schooling environment, there are significant demands on a child that requires the ability to self-regulate. We often ask children to control their desire to play, sit still, listen and attend to a specific activity (Cowley, 2021, p. 62). The interventions to develop self-soothing and self-regulation activities are to support this endeavour, but beyond that to also support infants and children as they develop into wider social circles.

HURTING OTHERS

When children find it difficult to manage their emotions they may hurt others. Hurting others is an act that may be intentional to cause harm, or entirely incidental and without malice. When a child intentionally hurts another to cause them pain, or perhaps because they are unable to control their frustration or anger, it can be a problematic issue to deal with in the classroom or school environment. Further challenges arise from difficulties in knowing what the specific cause of a child hurting another may be; there is no one reason to explain why children may have aggressive behaviour (Reebye, 2005). Instead, there are a range of reasons why a child may hurt other children. Reebye (2005) describes different pathways that may lead to a child being violent including individual reasons such as intrauterine trauma, differences in gender, temperament, family disturbances, exposure to violence, attachment and relation-ships, and neurodevelopmental reasons This huge number of potential reasons presents educators with challenges on how to support children effectively.

It is possible that you have direct experience of a child hurting another child. Perhaps your experience was as a parent being informed that your child had been bitten by another at nursery, or even that your child was the one that had bitten someone. It may be that, as someone who works in a schooling environment, you have witnessed or had to report a child hurting another or having been hurt. However, you may have no experience with any of the situations and thus to help with reflection on this difficult subject I have provided different examples to cover issues around bullying, and intentionally and unintentionally hurting others.

It is common for very young children to hurt others. Infants may hurt others at a higher rate than older children and adults (Dahl, 2016). The reason for a child hurting another varies. Some children may hurt another because they are frustrated (for example, to get a toy). Others may hurt children through responding to the aggression of others (hitting back) (Dahl, 2016). It appears that the use of force is linked to the acquisi-tion of language as well as cognitive and emotional skills that are required to regulate frustration (Dahl, 2016). There is likely a reduction in harming others not only as children develop the ability to communicate their frustrations but also as a result of negative reactions from their family, which reinforces how their individual actions may affect others (Dahl, 2016).

INTERVENTION AND SUPPORT FOR CHILDREN TO HELP MANAGE EMOTIONS

MANAGING EMOTIONS TOOL 1: BREATHING EXERCISES

Promote the use of activities that slow breathing to help a child co-regulate (Grimmer, 2022). The purpose of breathing exercises is to counteract some of the fast-paced breathing experienced when a child might be finding it difficult to control their emotions; it also serves as a distraction and redirection.

Activities which can help to slow down or control breathing include:

- blowing a feather across a table
- blowing up a balloon
- blowing the seeds of a dandelion flower
- blowing bubbles
- breathing like a dragon: take a deep breath through your nose and hold it for two seconds before exhaling with a roar

MANAGING EMOTIONS TOOL 2: HOME VISITS

Many of the interventions and strategies for children to develop self-soothing and self-regulation techniques include a key adult to be alongside the child. Sharing strategies across home and school is likely to be helpful, although it is important to remember that there are different demands in each setting, thus what you may see at school may not be seen in the home environment.

Young children benefit from knowing what a new setting might look like – this doesn't just refer to the physical environment, but the staff and the rules and routines. To begin this, if time and resources allow, home visits can be beneficial for all concerned. It can provide opportunities for parents/carers to raise concerns and tell you about their child. It is also a chance to tell parents/carers about some of the toys and books available in the new setting, or even provide information about nursery rhymes or songs that they sing (Cowley, 2021, p. 80). This can also be a time in which you can provide the names of any key workers, menus or other things that will support familiarity with the environment.

MANAGING EMOTIONS TOOL 3: USE OF CIRCLE TIME

Circle time is a group activity that is used to support younger children in developing positive relationships with one another. The purpose is to give children practice in a safe place to listen to one another, take turns and talk to one another. Circle time is not just an opportunity to converse freely, but it is also structured so that all children have an opportunity to participate.

Often the facilitator will start by ensuring that all children are aware of the ground rules. The ground rules may be co-created depending on the group setting or be an extension of classroom rules. They typically include aspects that help support turn-taking, valuing the contributions of all children and showing mutual respect. These will be presented and worded in a way that allows children to be able to clearly understand these ground rules.

As the name suggests, during circle time, the children and teacher will typically sit in a circle, and this can be either on the floor or on chairs. There should not be a power differential between the teacher and child, as the purpose is to encourage quieter members of the classroom to be able to speak within the group.

Traditionally, the use of an object symbolises a child's time to speak – these can be things such as a ball, a teddy or anything large enough to be seen from one side of the circle to the other. Within circle time, the teacher may support different games or activities to help develop participation. A particular issue that affects the class can be introduced and discussed. In the case of bullying, the approach to circle time could be as follows:

1 The children are reminded of the ground rules for circle time.
2 A warm-up activity could be singing "Head, Shoulders, Knees and Toes" and the children touching the relevant part of their body depending on the part of the song. Encourage listening skills by leaving out a word and having children respond by not touching the part that is omitted.
3 For the main activity, the teacher reads a story to the class about a child who is being bullied (for example, this could be *Monty the Manatee* by Natalie Pritchard or *Mud Boy: A Story about Bullying* by Sarah Siggs).
4 The teacher then passes around the symbolic object that establishes whose turn it is to talk. You can ask prompting questions such as how a character might feel in the book, or if they have noticed anything like this at school.

5 Try another activity that focuses on a different aspect where bullying has been noticed. for example, ask the pupils what games they like to play in the playground. Are there any games that are difficult to play? Are the rules complicated?

6 For the calming down activity, choose one your class is comfortable with, such as blowing bubbles, yoga or mindfulness exercise.

SUMMARY

- Self-regulation refers to an individual's ability to manage and control their emotions in socially appropriate ways.
- Co-regulation is the first step before children (or adults) can self-regulate.
- Self-regulation is a process that takes time to develop.

FURTHER RESOURCES

In the educational landscape, there is a deluge of resources that may be helpful for your own context. In this section, I explore the mapping of local support and consider other organisations that may support further help. I also signpost some resources that may be useful within your work as a teacher or support staff.

OTHER RESOURCES

Author/Organisation	Title/URL	Type of resource
Anxiety		
Virginia Ironside	*The Huge Bag of Worries*	Storybook
Cathy Creswell and Lucy Willetts	*Overcoming Your Child's Fears and Worries*	Self-help guide
Dr Karen Treisman	*Olly the Octopus*	Story and activity book
Bereavement		
Winston's Wish	www.winstonswish. org/	Website
Michael Rosen	*Sad Book*	Storybook
Dick Bruna	*Dear Grandma Bunny*	Storybook
Patrice Karst	*The Invisible String*	Storybook
Pat Thomas	*I Miss You*	Storybook
Dr Karen Treisman	*Binnie the Baboon*	Story and activity book *(Continued)*

DOI: 10.4324/9781003273097-15

Emotional regulation

Amanda Peddle	*TAMS Journey*	Storybooks
	The Beginning	
	The Middle	
	The End	
Dr Karen Treisman	*Cleo the Crocodile*	Story and
	Presley the Pug	activity
		books
Sarah Johnson	www.phoenixgrouphq. com/tools	Website

Harmful sexual behaviour

National Society for the Prevention of Cruelty to Children (NSPCC)	www.nspcc.org.uk/	Website
Barnado's	www.barnardos.org. uk/	Website
Stop It Now!	www.stopitnow.org. uk/	Website
Brook	www.brook.org.uk/	Website

MAPPING SCHOOL SUPPORT

As a fundamental approach, it is important to consider the support and key individuals within your local context. The resources (whether these are people, tools, community spaces or otherwise) are particular to specific contexts and can't necessarily be signposted within the context of a book with a wide audience.

Using the following as a framework, consider the individuals or organisations that you may draw upon to help you further develop your skills for children with SEMH. Consider whom you might add to the bullet points.

Universal support – the support available for all children throughout your organisation

- *For example, teachers*
-
-
-

Targeted support – the support that is available for individuals or groups that require some more support

- *For example, specific lessons on emotional regulation*
-
-
-
-

Specialised support – the specific support that is needed for individuals or small groups that require more focussed attention to have their needs met

- *For example, counselling, mentoring programme*
-
-
-

Next, beyond the school gates is likely to be additional resources. Throughout the book, I hope to have reiterated the role of parents/carers as well as the young people themselves, but depending on your context you may have access to third-sector resources (charity, grassroots organisations) as well as businesses that may be relevant. However, in mapping out this information it is important to find out some basic information about these organisations to ensure that the values and visions match with your own moral compass.

Some questions that might help you:

- How is the organisation funded?
- What are the values of the organisation?
- How are staff/volunteers recruited, and do they align with safeguarding/child protection?
- Does the organisation support all children or young people, or are there exceptions?
- What are these exceptions and what is the justification for them?

Finally, consider some of the references pointed to within this book. From the beginning, it is important to have a broad overview of child development; how children learn and grow can be fundamental to understanding how we can teach to their age and stage, and in a way that ensures that children feel and are safe. These may be explored through the use of storytelling, specific training, or growing your professional learning network through face-to-face opportunities or perhaps social media outlets such as Twitter or LinkedIn.

MAPPING RESOURCES WITHIN AND BEYOND THE SCHOOL GATES

The image that follows is some ideas on how you might begin to map your own resources within the school and wider community. You can utilise an incomplete version of this to be able to explore as a wider staff team. As it will be particular to your own setting, you can also include the name of organisations or any resources that you purchase specifically to support SEND. With this, you can start to have a sense of what is available within your setting, or perhaps what you think might enhance what you already have.

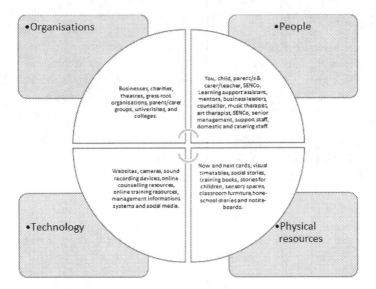

None of the tools offered under each section can work in isolation. The phrase "it takes a village to raise a child" is an important one: it asserts the need for the community to draw together to support a child. Interventions and support within the school are important to ensure that a child belongs and is supported. But without drawing upon the assets and resources of those around the child and the wider school community, it will be harder to fully support children and their families when things are difficult.

BIBLIOGRAPHY

About selective mutism. (2022, March 12). Selective mutism. Retrieved from http://www.selectivemutism.org.uk/about -selective-mutism/

Ainsworth, M., & Wittig, B. (1969). Attachment and exploratory behavior of one-year-olds in a strange situation. In B. M. Foss (Ed.), *Determinants of infant behavior* (Vol. 4, pp. 113-136). Hoboken, NJ: Wiley.

Allardyce, S., & Yates, P. (2018). *Working with children and young people who have displayed harmful sexual behaviour.* London: Dunedin.

American Psychiatric Association. (1968). *Diagnostic and statistical manual of mental disorders* (2nd ed.). Washington: American Psychiatric Publishing.

American Psychiatric Association. (2013). *Diagnostic and statistical manual of mental disorders* (5th ed.). Washington: American Psychiatric Publishing. https://doi.org/10.1176/ appi.books.9780890425596

Ansorge, R. 'Piaget Stages of Development', WebMD.com, https:// www.webmd.com/children/piaget-stages-of-development

Asquith, S. (2020). *Self-regulation skills in young children.* London: Jessica Kingsley Publishers.

Bateman, J., & Milner, J. (2015). *Children and young people whose behaviour is sexually concerning or harmful: Assessing risk and developing safety plans.* London: Jessica Kingsley Publishers.

Black, B., & Uhde, T. W. (1995). Psychiatric characteristics of children with selective mutism: A pilot study. *Journal of the American Academy of Child and Adolescent Psychiatry, 34*(7), 847-856.

Blackburn, C., Carpenter, B., & Egerton, J. (2012). *Educating children and young people with fetal alcohol spectrum disorders: Constructing personalised pathways to learning.* Oxon: Routledge.

Bombèr, L. M. (2020). *Know me to teach me.* Broadway, UK: Worth Publishing.

Bombèr, L. M. (2021). *Inside I'm hurting: Practical strategies for supporting children with attachment difficulties in schools.* Croydon: Worth Publishing.

Bowlby, J. (1969). *Attachment (volume 1 of Attachment and Loss).* London: Hogarth Press.

Brook. (2022, July 15). *Sexual behaviours traffic light tool.* Brook.org.uk. Retrieved from https://www.brook.org.uk/training/wider-professional-training/sexual-behaviours-traffic-light-tool/

Brooks, R. (2020). *The trauma and attachment aware classroom.* London: Jessica Kingsley Publishers.

Buron, K. D., & Curtis, M. (2012). *The incredible 5-point scale: The significantly improved and expanded* (2nd ed.). Shawnee, KS: AAPC Publishing.

Cowley, S. (2021). *Learning behaviours: A practical guide to self-regulation in the early years.* London: John Catt Publication.

Dahl, A. (2016). Infants' unprovoked acts of force towards others. *Developmental Science, 19*(6), 1049–1057.

Department for Education. (2020). *Special educational needs in England: January 2020.* Explore Education Statistics. Retrieved from https://explore-education-statistics.service.gov.uk/find-statistics/special-educational-needs-in-england/2019-20

Department for Education, Department for Health. (2022, February 07). Gov.uk. Retrieved from https://assets.publishing.service.gov.uk/government/uploads/system/uploads/attachment_data/file/398815/SEND_Code_of_Practice_January_2015.pdf

Draugedalen, K. (2019). Teachers' responses to harmful sexual behaviour in primary school – Findings from a digital survey among primary school teachers. *Journal of Sexual Aggression, 27*(2), 233–246.

Duke University. (2016). *Difficulties with mathematics.* Understanding fetal alcohol spectrum disorders. Retrieved

April 12, 2022, from https://sites.duke.edu/fasd/chapter
-5-the-fasd-student-and-learning-issues/difficulties-with
mathematics/

Ey, L.-A., McInnes, E., & Rigney, L.-I. (2017). Educators'
understanding of young children's typical and problematic
sexual behaviour and their training in this area. *Sexuality,
Society and Learning*, *17*(6), 682–696.

FASD Toolkit. (2022, April 4). *Social stories*. FASD toolkit.
Retrieved from https://fasdtoolkit.weebly.com/social-stories.
html

Fitzpatrick, C. (2012). *A short introduction to understanding
and supporting children and young people who self-harm*.
London: Jessica Kingsley Publishers.

Gothenburg University. (2020, August 30). *Lecture on PANDAS
with Dr Susan Swedo*. Gilbery Neuropsychiatry Centre.
Retrieved from https://www.gu.se/en/gnc/lecture-on
-pandas-with-dr-susan-swedo

Gov.uk. (2022, March 25). *Definition of disability under the
Equality Act 2010*. Gov.uk. Retrieved from https://www.gov.
uk/definition-of-disability-under-equality-act-2010

Gray, C. (2015). *It is not a social story if...a screening tool*. Carol
Gray Social Stories. Retrieved April 4, 2022, from https://car
olgraysocialstories.com/wp-content/uploads/2015/09/It-is
-NOT-a-Social-Story-if....pdf

Gray, C. (2022, April 4). *What is a social story?* Carol Gray Social
Stories. Retrieved from https://carolgraysocialstories.com/
social-stories/what-is-it

Grimmer, T. (2022). *Supporting behaviour and emotions in the
early years*. Oxon: Routledge.

Grover, N. (2020, September 29). A quarter of adopted UK
Children affected by drinking during pregnancy. *The Guardian*.
Retrieved from https://www.theguardian.com/society
/2020/sep/29/a-quarter-of-adopted-uk-children-affected
-by-drinking-during-pregnancy#:~:text=Among%20the
%20adopters%20surveyed%20by,as%20behavioural
%20and%20learning%20difficulties

Guyon-Harris, K. L., Humphreys, K. L., Miron, D., Gleason, M. M.,
Nelson, C. A., Fox, N. A., & Zeanah, C. H. (2019). Disinhibited
social engagement disorder in early childhood predicts
reduced competence in early adolescence. *Journal of
Abnormal Psychology*, *47*(10), 1735–1745.

Hoffman, J. (2019, February 12). Words matter – Why self-soothing is one of the most misapplied terms in child development. Self-Regulation Institute. Retrieved from https://selfregulationinstitute.org/2019/02/12/words-matter-why-self-soothing-is-one-of-the-most-misapplied-terms-in-child-development/

Holka-Pokorska, J., Piróg-Balcerzak, A., & Jarema, M. (2018). The controversy around the diagnosis of selective mutism – A critical analysis of three cases in the light of modern research and diagnostic criteria. *Psychiatria Polska*, *52*(2), 323–343. doi: 10.12740/PP/76088

Honig, A. S., & Zdunowski-Sjoblom, N. (2013). Bullied children: Parent and school supports. *Early Child Development and Care*, *184*(9–10), 1378–1402.

Jellinek, M. S. (May 2010). Don't let ADHD crush children's self-esteem. *Clinical Psychiatry News*, *38*(5), 12. DOI:10.1016/S0270-6644(10)70231-9

Kokanovic, I., & Barron, I. (2021). Efficacy of EMDR: Case study of a child with choking phobia – Case report. *Psychiatria Dunubine*, *33*(1), 33–41.

Kuypers, L. M. (2011). *The zones of regulation: A curriculum designed to foster self-regulation and emotional control.* San Jose, CA: Think Social Publishing.

Langton, E. G., & Frederickson, N. (2018). Parents' experiences of professionals' involvement for children with extreme demand avoidance. *International Journal of Developmental Disabilities*, *64*(1), 16–24.

Lloyd, J. (2019). Response and intervention into harmful sexual behaviour in schools. *Child Abuse and Neglect*, *94*.

Lovino, E. B., Koslouski, J. B., & Chafouleas, S. M. (2021). Teaching simple strategies to foster emotional well-being. *Frontiers in Psychology.* https://doi.org/10.3389/fpsyg.2021.772260

Mainstone-Cotton, S. (2021). *Supporting children with social, emotional and mental health needs in the early years: Practical solutions and strategies for every setting.* Oxon: Routledge.

Marshall, N. (2014). *The teacher's introduction to attachment: Practical essentials for teachers, carers and school support staff.* London: Jessica Kingsley Publishers.

Moore, A. (2020). Pathological demand avoidance: What and who are being pathologised and in whose interests?

Psychiatrised Childhoods: Observed, Understood and Experienced, 10(1), 39–52. Retrieved March 31, 2022, https://journals.sagepub.com/doi/full/10.1177/2043610619890070

Mueller, A. K., Tucha, L., Koerts, J., & Fuermaier, A. B. (2012). Stigma in attention deficit hyperactivity disorder. *Attention Deficit and Hyperactivity Disorders*, 101–114.

National Institute of Mental Health. (2022, February 18). *PANDAS – Questions and answers*. Transforming the understanding and treatment of mental illness. Retrieved from https://www.nimh.nih.gov/health/publications/pandas#:~:text=PANDAS%20is%20short%20for%20Pediatric,strep%20throat%20or%20scarlet%20fever

NHS Ayrshire and Arran. (2022, April 04). *Understanding fetal alcohol spectrum disorder: What educators need to know*. Retrieved from https://www.nhsaaa.net, https://www.nhsaaa.net/media/8391/fasd_whateducatorsneedtoknow.pdf

NOFASD Australia. (2022, April 11). *Managing challenge or extreme behaviour*. NOFASD Australia. Retrieved from https://www.nofasd.org.au/managing-challenging-and-or-extreme-behaviour/

Office for National Statistics (2022). Academic year 2021/22: Special educational needs in England. https://explore-education-statistics.service.gov.uk/find-statistics/special-educational-needs-in-england/2021-22

Ollendick, T. H., King, N. J., & Miris, P. (2002). Fears and phobias in children: Phenomenology, epidemiology, and aetiology. *Children and Adolescent Mental Health*, 10, 98–106.

Omdal, H. (2008). Including children with selective mutism in mainstream schools and kindergarten: Problems and possibilities. *International Journal of Inclusive Education*, 12(3), 301–315.

Ory, N. E. (2022, April 11). *How to divert someone you cannot confront without an explosion?* NOFASD Australia. Retrieved from https://static.fasdoutreach.ca/www/downloads/divert.pdf

Özurk Dönmez, R., & Bayik Temel, A. (2019). Effect of soothing techniques on infants' self-regulation behaviors (sleeping, crying, feeding): A randomized controlled study. *Japan Journal of Nursing Science*, 16(4), 407–419.

Padmore, J. (2016). *The mental health needs of children and young people*. Berkshire: McGraw Publishers; Open University Press.

Reebye, P. (2005). Aggression during early years – Infancy and preschool. *Canadian Child and Adolescent Psychiatry Review*, *14*(1), 16–20.

Ryan, C. (n.d.). ADHD and Me. https://chatterpack.net/products/adhd-and-me

Scheeringa , M. (2022, April 16). *PTSD for children 6 years and younger*. US Department of Veteran Affairs. Retrieved from https://www.ptsd.va.gov/professional/treat/specific/ptsd_child_under6.asp

Seim, A. R., Jozefiak, T., Wichstrøm, L., Lydersen, S., & Kayed, N. S. (2021). Self-esteem in adolescents with reactive attachment disorder or disinhibited social engagement disorder. *Child abuse & neglect*, *118*, 105141. https://doi.org/10.1016/j.chiabu.2021.105141

Southham-Gerow, M. A. (2016). *Emotional regulation in children and adolescents: A practitioner's guide*. London: The Guildford Press.

Special educational needs and disability code of practice 0–25 years. (2005, January). Department for Education, Department of Health.

Substance Abuse and Mental Health Services Administration. (n.d.). DSM-5 changes: Implications for child serious emotional disturbance. Retrieved January 12, 2022, from https://www.ncbi.nlm.nih.gov/books/NBK519712

Tedeschi, F. K., & Billick, S. B. (2017). Pediatric PTSD in the DSM-5 and the forensic interview of traumatized youth. *Journal of the American Academy of Psychiatry and the Law Online*, *45*(2), 175–183.

Thambirajah, M. S., De-Hayes, L., & Grandinson, K. J. (2007). *Understanding school refusal: A handbook for professionals in education, health and social care*. London: Jessica Kingsley Publishers.

Thierry, B. D. (2017). *The simple guide to child trauma: What it is and how to help*. London: Jessica Kingsley Publishers.

UNICEF. (2022, March 25). *How we protect children's rights with the UN Convention on the Rights of the Child*. UNICEF. Retrieved from https://www.unicef.org.uk/what-we-do/un-convention-child-rights/

US Department of Education. (2006). *Teaching children with attention deficit hyperactivity disorder: Instructional strategies and practices*. US Department of Education. Washington, DC: ED Pubs, Education Publications Center.

Retrieved February 15, 2022, from https://files.eric.ed.gov/fulltext/ED495483.pdf

Very Well Mind. (2022, February 22). *DSM 5 criteria for generalised anxiety disorder*. Very well mind. Retrieved from https://www.verywellmind.com/dsm-5-criteria-for-generalized-anxiety-disorder-1393147

What is self-soothing? Learn about this important social-emotional tool. (2022, April 16). Pathways.org. Retrieved from https://pathways.org/self-soothing/

White, J., Bond, C., & Carroll, C. (2022). An exploration of how selective mutism training informs teachers' understanding and practice. *Support for Learning, 37*(1), 3–20.

Whitters, H. G. (2021). *Adverse childhood experiences, attachment, and the early years learning environment*. Oxon: Routledge Focus.

Williams, C. E., Bishop, F. L., & Hadwin, J. A. (2021). Primary teachers' experiences of teaching pupils with selective mutism: A grounded theory study. *Educational Psychology in Practice, 37*(3), 267–283.

World Health Organization. (2022, January). *ICD-11*. ICD-11 for mortality and morbidity statistics. Retrieved from https://icd.who.int/browse11/l-m/en#/http://id.who.int/icd/entity/1877502096

Printed in the United States
by Baker & Taylor Publisher Services